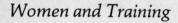

Women and Training

OPEN UNIVERSITY PRESS
Gender and Education Series

Editors

ROSEMARY DEEM

*Lecturer in the School of Education at the
Open University*

GABY WEINER

*Course Manager in the School of Education at the
Open University*

The series provides compact and clear accounts of relevant research and practice in the field of gender and education. It is aimed at trainee and practising teachers, and parents and others with an educational interest in ending gender inequality. All age-ranges will be included, and there will be an emphasis on ethnicity as well as gender. Series authors are all established educational practitioners or researchers.

TITLES IN THE SERIES

Women and Training

Ann Wickham

Open University Press
Milton Keynes • Philadelphia

Open University Press
Open University Educational Enterprises Limited
12 Cofferidge Close
Stony Stratford
Milton Keynes MK11 1BY, England

and
242 Cherry Street
Philadelphia, PA 19106, USA

First Published 1986

British Library Cataloguing in Publication Data

Wickham, Ann
   Women and training. —— (Gender and education)
   1. Women —— Training of —— Great Britain
   2. Sex discrimination against women —— Great Britain
   I. Title II. Series
   331.4'133'0941   HD6059.6.G7

   ISBN 0-335-15119-1

Library of Congress Cataloging in Publication Data

Main entry under title:
Wickham, Ann.
   Women and Training.
   (Gender and Education Series)
   Bibliography: P.
   Includes Index.
   1. Occupational Training for Women —— Great Britain.
   2. Women —— Employment —— Great Britain.
   3. Women —— Education (Secondary) —— Great Britain.
   I. Title. II. Series.
   HD 6059.6.G7W52   1986   331.4'2592'0941   86-5176

   ISBN 0-335-15119-1

Text design by Clarke Williams
Typeset by Colset Pte Ltd, Singapore
Printed in Great Britain by St. Edmondsbury Press,
Bury St. Edmunds, Suffolk

CONTENTS

Series Editors' Introduction

Ann Wickham's book appears at a point when the whole issue of women's employment is a major area of political debate. Employment is increasingly becoming the norm for all adult women under 60 in the UK, with breaks taken for childrearing becoming shorter. At the same time, women remain heavily concentrated in a few sectors of the labour market, many married women are in part-time rather than full-time employment, and the nature of jobs in general is changing rapidly. So the question of training opportunities is vital, all the more so because as earlier books in the series have shown, education up to 18 is still much pervaded by sexism and gender segregation.

What this book does is to draw our attention to how far behind contemporary thinking, training facilities and opportunities for women have lagged, to the extent that the level of awareness about sexism and gender discrimination are even lower than in many sectors of formal schooling. Such training as does exist tends either to ignore the labour market, or to take the existing gender segregation of the labour market for granted, ignores women's continuing domestic and child-care burdens and has almost failed to notice black women at all. Ann Wickham both examines the reasons behind this (for example the links between masculinity and notions of skill and the continuing patriarchal dominance of men in decision-making about training) and the industrial development of training in Britain. She examines the present provision available for school leavers through the Manpower Services Commission in further education and for women returners, and provides some useful insights into the training facilities and opportunities available in other industrial societies, principally the USA, USSR and Sweden. Her final chapter looks at some of the lessons which can be drawn from her disturbing analysis of the relationship between education, training and the labour market, not only for training agencies but also for employers and central and local government too. She points the way towards an 'active and invigorating' training policy for women. This book will be highly relevant not only to those involved with providing training opportunities, but also to secondary school teachers, politicians and women seeking or currently undertaking training themselves.

Rosemary Deem
Gaby Weiner

Introduction

In a period of increasing unemployment and deep recession training has become what it never was before, a central political issue. Social disorder, whether at football matches or in the streets of the inner cities, is linked in the media and in political debate to the rising unemployment figures. Vandalism, crime and hard drug-taking are all regarded as responses to the lack of any meaningful future. Training has become linked into this scenario because it is through training people that it is hoped some will find jobs or gain the skills that will help them generate employment in co-operatives or small businesses. Training is also seen as a way of helping those made redundant as the deindustrialisation of much of Britain continues. However, this concentration on training as some form of panacea to a variety of social ills breeds further problems: at least it does as far as women are concerned.

If gangs of youths are seen rioting in the streets these shadowy figures are men. If there is a heart-rending picture of unemployment the image that springs first to mind is that of the man leaning disconsolately against the wall at the street corner whilst children play at his feet. Throughout this century the problem of employment and unemployment has always been one that involved men rather than women. Women may make up a large percentage of the labour force, they may lose jobs or future opportunities just as easily as men, but women have never been seen as a political problem. Maybe part of this is because their forms of resistance and self-definition are seldom regarded as creating any serious social threat. As a result, when training programmes are being developed they are aimed mainly at groups which although categorised as 'youth' or 'redundant workers' etc. are seen mainly as involving men.

We live in a society which is stratified, but there are other deep and serious divisions bar those of class. Ethnic and gender divisions cross-cut those of class but they are seldom taken into account in policy making in any serious fashion even when the rhetoric is present. What I try to do in this book is look at the development of different forms of training in Britain and ask how far these meet the needs of women. To this extent I too am concentrating on one particular division in our society though this could not exclude consideration of ethnic and class differences. I look at women as a group because I believe, and I hope the book shows, that most of the training opportunities available at the moment are unsuitable for most women, and that what we need is a far more active, interventionary programme than any we have at present. Women from different classes or different ethnic groups have other problems to face and I try to deal with some of these but there are common problems that all women share, just because they are women, and it is on these I mainly concentrate. In part this is also a result of the available material. There is very little material as yet about the problems faced by ethnic groups in our societies, especially in the area of training. Much of what is produced tends to treat groups of men and women as having the same interests because they belong to the same ethnic group. Yet there is evidence to show that this is just not so in many areas and it would be surprising if training were any different. Therefore the problems of ethnicity remain a theme for this book but one that is not developed so strongly and fully as we really require.

I start in Chapter I by discussing the exclusion of women from many areas of training and the links between definitions of masculinity and technology and skill which have helped to perpetrate this situation. Chapters 2 and 3 trace the historical development of training in Britain and the problems created in developing a more responsive training policy for women by regional differences, ethnic differences and the advent of new technology. Chapters 4, 5 and 6 look in more detail at the kind of training opportunities that are available in Britain and ask how far they are suitable for the needs of women. Chapter 4 examines youth programmes, particularly those of the Manpower Services Commission. Chapter 5 concentrates on further education and the training opportunities available in that sector as well as the kind of opportunities available post school and within employment. Chapter 6 looks at one particular group of women and their training problems, women who have had a break from paid employment and now wish to re-enter the labour market.

Examination of these various sectors rapidly leads to the conclusion that there still remains a great deal to be done if women are to get effective opportunities in training. Chapter 7 therefore looks at examples from other countries, the USA, Sweden and the USSR, to see if any of the changes there, particularly legislatively-based ones, would be suitable to help transform the situation in Britain. The final chapter draws together the points from throughout the book and tries to sketch out what a training policy that did suit the needs of women might look like. It also explores examples of good practice which illustrate the kinds of immediate changes that could be introduced into existing programmes and which could help to extend women's opportunities.

CHAPTER 1

Defining the Problem

My mother worked in an office, my female cousin works in a shop, my sister-in-law is a primary-school teacher. There are very few men employed in the places where they work. I work as a lecturer but in the department where I work only one of the permanent staff is female the rest are men. The director of the institution I work in and all his senior administrative staff are men, as are all the heads of departments. Our everyday experiences tell us what national statistical confirm, that men and women tend to do very different jobs, that occupations are 'feminised' or 'masculinised', In the same way we know that not many women are found in positions of importance or responsibility, and that this can often occur even when women make up the majority in that job. Many primary school teachers are women, for example, but the smaller number of men in that occupation have a much better chance of becoming heads of primary schools that any of the women.

One, but only one, of the explanations for this situation is that women have not had access to training that would either let them enter a particular occupation or give them access to positions of importance or promotion witin an occupation. Some people would prefer to think that this was just a problem for individual women, that women can't be bothered and training because 'all they're interested in is clothes, having a good time then getting married'. It's simpler to think that it's a problem for individuals than to ask questions as to why women aren't getting the training that would give them promotion. In the same way many would prefer to see it as 'natural' that men and women do different jobs, that men have strength and attributes of leadership and women the dexterity, emotion and feeling that make them suited for different types of work. The universality of such assumptions is easily exploded by the way that different societies or different cultures assign men and women different characteristics as men and as women. In some cultures, for example, it is thought women are best suited to heavy manual labour. Even in our own society attitudes have changed over time. Women and children used to work in the mines, one of the areas of work most often associated with muscle power and strength. It is also interesting to reflect why women are still associated with weakness when they can be seen any day of the week struggling down high streets all over Britain with toddlers, babies, buggies, bags of shopping, a combination that any parent will tell you requires considerable physical resources. On other occasions the same occupation can be dominated by men in one society and by women in another society (e.g. being a general practitioner). It becomes important, then, to explain why women in our society aren't getting access to the forms of training that might open up new jobs and occupations and which would allow them to be promoted. We can no longer assume that this is just the way life is and that women happily collude in this situation. If this situation is not a 'natural' one, if men's and women's position at different levels and in different occupations is the result of social rather than biological factors, then we can examine the process through which this patterning occurs. We can ask what part training has to play in the process of differentiation which discriminates against women and we can ask what it is possible to do to change this situation.

Training is one of the ways which are used to monitor entry into occupations. You can't become a doctor or an engineer, a carpenter or a car mechanic without some form of training. Once in a job you often can't be promoted without some form of training, in banks for example. It is therefore very important that women have access to forms of training which will give them opportunities for either entry or promotion. It is equally important that the forms of training offered do not reproduce or reinforce the present structure of gender inequalities in paid employment. Chapters of this book will therefore look at the different forms of training that are available and will argue that women are often systematically excluded from them or discriminated against once within them.

Of course, it is clear that many women leave school without the qualifications that allow them the entry to certain forms of training. Many women, for instance, lack the qualifications in maths and science that are necessary to get into training schemes at many technical institutions. Today there are efforts being made by individual teachers as well as education authorities and other agencies to direct women into these subject areas whilst they are at school. This is one solution to the problem but not the only one. It is not impossible, for instance to recognise that this situation occurs in schools *and* to build compensatory introductions into training programmes. On other occasions it is argued that it wouldn't matter how much women got access to training programmes because, whilst qualifications can act as entry requirements for occupations, they don't ensure access and other forms of discrimination can operate to ensure that women aren't taken on for jobs. This may be true in some cases but it does not apply in all cases. There are many occupations, especially those where qualifications gained after getting a job are important, where increased access to training opportunities would help women get the promotion and opportunities that they deserve.

Until fairly recently education and training have been seen as different things and to some extent the distinction still holds. Education has been regarded as the general development of knowledge, understanding and values. It is something that takes place in schools in our society, and in which all children are required to participate (unless there are very special circumstances) until their mid-teens. Training, on the other hand, is usually seen as a process of acquisition of certain competencies, of specific vocational skills which will be used in paid employment. This training can be undertaken in colleges, in special skill centres or at work. It is the kind of process that we have always associated with apprenticeships, for example, even though training can also be undertaken in a fairly informal fashion, 'sitting next to Nellie'.

Whilst education and training have been kept fairly distinct in the past, this does not mean that the two are not related. Access to training schemes can rely on family links and this has often been the case with apprenticeships, but increasingly formal educational qualifications have been used to limit entry into training schemes. This situation has worked to the disadvantage of many women who, in many cases, have not got the formal educational requirements that are demanded. This is especially the case with technical or scientific occupations where women have not acquired the maths or science qualifications that are desired. Whilst all children, male and female, get schooling not all have access to training. But it is the women who are worst off at every level and in every sort of training. Whether we look at apprenticeships, at further education courses and off-the-job training, or even internal training within firms the picture is always the same, women always represent the smallest percentage in the training programmes overall. In individual areas they may dominate, for example in day release for hairdressing, but this is the exceptional situation for the second characteristic of training is the fact that training tends to be provided in occupations where there are not a lot of women.

How has this occurred? Is it just that women aren't interested in training? Some people might like to think so, especially those who attitudes are founded on a belief that woman's place is in the home. Yet all the evidence, in fact, points to other factors. Is this just accidental? If it were just the fact that women weren't on training schemes when they could be then this might be so. It is quite clear that schooling is gender-specific, that is it teaches males and females different things. This is not just a case of what subjects boys and girl actually take at school although that is part of the problem. We know that in the past boys have been encouraged to do woodwork and science subjects, for example, whilst the girls have been directed towards domestic science, and if into a science into biology rather than physics or chemistry. It is this subject routing that has left many women in the past unable to gain access into training schemes which require the kind of subject qualifications they just don't have and haven't had the opportunity to acquire. But it is also the case that schools teach more than that. In the classroom children acquire knowledge of what is suitable behaviour for boys and for girls. Studies of classrooms show that teachers behave differently to boys and to girls, they speak to them differently, they require different responses and different behaviour from them. Children don't just learn History and English they also learn what is expected of them as males and as females. These demands may even be subtly moderated to match for example, what is required of a child from a working-class background rather than a middle-class one, from a rural area rather than an urban one. In this situation many females acquire the 'femininity' which shapes their aspirations, which makes them look to marriage not the labour market as their future, to childrearing rather than time in a job, even though in practice this is far from being the situation in society. In Britain since the Second World War we have seen the massive expansion of the numbers of women in paid employment. Very few women these days withdraw entirely from the labour market at marriage or even when the children are born, and each year increasing numbers are re-entering the labour market after a break for children (Martin and Roberts, 1984).

The end result of this situation has been a lack of interest in training by many women who at school have learnt to value the goals of femininity rather than make any realistic assessment of their likely future. They neither challenge the masculine dominance of certain occupations nor question their lack of access to fields of knowledge which are also seen as 'male'. With no future in view apart from marriage and children they do not look to break into male occupations nor seek promotion within the spheres they enter. Problems such as these have to be faced in the schools and already there are many efforts being made to mitigate this situation and to attract girls into 'male' subjects, and therefore also open up the possibilities of new forms of paid employment for them. The WISE year (Women into Science and Engineering) sponsored by the

Equal Opportunities Commission in 1984 was an attempt to do just this. However, there still remains a great deal to be done. Research suggests that much of the socialisation that occurs through education happens as much in the primary schools as in secondary level education and that much of it appears to be unconsciously implemented by the teachers. It is obvious, therefore, that there is still a great deal that will have to be undertaken in the area of teacher training and in developing self-awareness and self-monitoring in teachers. Many teachers may even resist such changes where they too are the products of the systems which has laid such stress on what is 'the right work for women'.

However, if we can talk about the development of femininity in girls as a general process, it also has to be recognised that that femininity will be structured by class and racial divisions. The expectations of what a woman can and cannot do in terms of occupation and career will differ. More girls than boys stay on at school but then there are more males than females in third-level education and this reflects assumptions about women and their life and level. More of the women found in third-level institutions are from middle-class backgrounds. In Britain, for example, the development of a grants system and the introduction of comprehensive education have still not altered the close links between the education hierarchy and the general class hierarchy. Of course, there will always be exceptions. Some working-class girls will make it to university, just as some girls will happily study maths and science subjects, indeed will fight for the chance to do so. However, these exceptions only serve to confirm the general picture. Femininity retains its impact, but the content and implications of that femininity is modulated through class position. Far more middle-class women are expected to have a dual role, a career and a family, these days rather than just the family as in the past, therefore more of them are expected to do 'A' levels and go on to higher education or college.

If there are differences in the impact of femininity and the content of that concept by class so too are there differences according to ethnic group. Early studies, for instance, talked about the labelling of Afro-Caribbean children in school so that they, their language and background were persistently devalued by the existing school system. But other studies have begun to suggest that this is too simple a categorisation and has to be broken down; there are major differences between male and female Afro-Caribbean children in the way that they react to school and the kind of value they place on academic achievement. Driver (1977) has suggested that female Afro-Caribbean students place a higher value on formal academic achievement and see it as a way of getting better jobs, and that this itself is something they desire. These aspirations are linked to the values of their mothers and the important role that Afr-Carribbean mothers play as breadwinners for their families.

However, if femininity is being produced in the schools so too is masculinity. As Paul Willis has shown in his study of boys at school (Willis, 1977) part of the process through which working-class boys subsequently end up in working-class jobs is the way in which they embrace a particular category of maleness, of what is involved in 'being a man'. In their case this leads to a devaluation of formal educational qualifications and a denial of the ethos of schools, and instead places value on the informal relationships of the workplace.

But masculinity involves much more than just the acquisition of beliefs about men's and women's characteristics, that men are strong and tough, unemotional and undomestic. Such beliefs lie behind the call for a family wage for a man who should always be the family breadwinner whilst the woman's place is in the home. But the concept of masculinity in our society is also linked to the ways in which we think about areas such as technology and skill and the way in which these have been defined and developed. Feminist work which suggested that masculinity was linked to such issues (Phillips and Taylor, 1980) has been followed by empirical studies of various occupations which document the way in which this link is made. More than that, they also show the way in which this linkage systematically excludes women from occupations, from promotion and from training.

Technology, the world of machines, has always in the West been part of an historical and ideological dualism, a split between a world of machines, a world of men, and that other world, that of women:

> The world of men is seen as disciplined and and demanding, and concerned with Important Things. The world of women is one of emotions and spontaneity. Here the technological man finds rest, admiration and inspiration for future deeds.
>
> (Berner, 1983)

Even when the complete seperation of those two worlds no longer applies so distinctly, when women do get to work with machines in paid employment, a dualism still persists. It persists in the segregation of women into lower levels of technology and into specialised areas. Women become the receivers and the operators of machinery, but never the controllers. Men and machines go hand in hand whilst women become seen as socially incompatible with technology.

> From the spanner to the lathe, the tools and the occupations associated with them were men's. Concomitants of electromechanical technologies were (part material, part ideological) 'dirt' and demands on 'strength'. The way femininity is socially constructed combines with the nature of electro-mechanical technology to make it incompatible with women.
>
> (Cockburn, 1984).

Technology has been historically shaped in the male image. All the things that are associated with machinery – dirt, noise, strength, all such images are ones that we have learnt to associate with males rather than females even if there are, in practice, women who work in dirty, difficulty and exhausting jobs. Socially these things are not seen as part of 'women's work'. Technology becomes imprinted with masculinity and to this extent women are actively being repelled by it (Cockburn, 1983). Women are not entering technological occupations in large numbers, not just because they as individuals don't 'like' such jobs and because they come out of school without the qualifications that they might need to enter such occupations – they are also being actively rejected by the masculinity of technology. Nor is it merely the case that machines are associated with conditions that are male: the machines themselves are constructed and designed with the male and not the female body and physiology in mind. Difference becomes inferiority when this happens. In many cases the machines themselves exclude female operators by the way in which they are made to work when alternative ways of achieving the same task would not be impossible.

> Many women have observed that mechanical equipment is manufactured and assembled in ways that make it just too big or too heavy for the 'average' woman to use. This need not be conspiracy, it is merely the outcome of a pre-existing pattern of power. It is a complex point. Women vary in bodily strength and size; they also vary in orientation, some having learned more confidence and more capability than others. Many processes could be carried out with machines designed to suit smaller or less muscular operators or reorganised so as to come within reach of the 'average' women.   (Cockburn, 1981)

However, if technology itself can be seen to have been shaped historically only in relation to male attributes and men's bodies, need this situation continue? Many feminists would answer 'yes' to such a question. For the masculine shaping of technology, it is argued, is related to the maintenance of men's own superior position on the labour market vis-a-vis women in general, and is also implicated in divisions and hierarchies amongst male workers, although the latter may be changing under the impact of new forms of technology.

The relationship between men and technology is such that machines are perceived as masculine. In the past many of the jobs involved with machines were regarded as craft jobs for men. They involved the acquisition of knowledge and skills related to the machine. Today many of these jobs (for example printing) are being de-skilled. That means that much of the judgement and knowledge as well as control of the work process that was once inherent in the worker is now being built into the machines. This is not a simple process nor is it one that goes uncontested by workers but it has happened in many places and male workers are left with repetitive and stationary tasks. Yet it can be argued that such is the relationship between men and technology that although men are left with unsatisfactory work tasks they are still able to salvage something from this situation:

Male workers are able to represent the power of the machine as
theirs and experience themselves as having 'technical' expertise. They can then measure their jobs against women's non-
technical jobs. The machine symbolises masculinity and
enables them to live out fantasies about power and domination which in turn reproduce this connection.

(Game and Pringle, 1984, p. 36).

The measurement of themselves against women is not just a
question of male egos and attitudes but has material effects as
well. Because they are tied to the machines the 'expertise'
becomes the basis for unequal pay and helps tie women to the
lower income occupations. If women move into 'male' areas
they are made to feel awkward and fit in only by becoming
'one of the boys', a result that is frequently found in studies of
women trying to move into areas such as engineering. At times
the exclusion of women will take the form of sexual harassment. Men who do 'women's work' may be seen as weak and
possibly effeminate and it is noticeable that when men do
move into areas of such work this tends to result in rapid
promotion for them, even over the heads of existing female
workers with more experience.

However, the links between men and machines are perhaps
at their strongest around manual work, although increasingly
such arguments can be applied around new technology. Non-
manual work, what is called 'mental' labour, has been, in
practice, superior in status and economic rewards to much
work with machines, so that we can see divisions between men
created by this relationship to technology. This picture will be
further complicated by the growth of occupations for men
associated with computing and other forms of information
technology. These will inherit the mantle of masculinity associated with technical work, but will have different conditions
of work and a different status to the old patterns of occupations associated with machinery. The dark-suited systems
analyst is unlikely ever to be regarded in the same way as the
oil-covered mechanic.

Control of technology is also closely related to questions of
skill. However, skill, is not just a concept related to machines
it also is involved in areas such as office work where we talk

of secretarial skills or management skills, for instance. Skills are something that we think of as being related to work. Apprentices, for instance, whether in carpentry, hairdressing, car mechanics or the myriad other areas of work with apprenticeships attached, are expected to acquire the skills necessary to become full practitioners of their craft. However, the concept of skill is a little more complex than that:

> skill itself . . . consists in at least three things. There is the skill that resides in the man himself, accumulated over time, each new experience adding something to the total ability. There is the skill demanded by the job – which may or may not match the skill in the worker. And there is the political definition of skill: that which a group of workers or a trade union can successfully defend against the challenge of employers and other groups of workers.   (Cockburn, 1983, p. 113).

The distinguishing of these different elements caught up in the notion of skill is very important when it comes to analysing the situation for women on the labour market. Whilst all three elements of skill were more or less coterminous for workers in the nineteenth century, numerous studies have shown that during the twentieth century this situation has changed. Employers have introduced or attempted to introduce changes in the labour process, in the actual practice of working, which no longer demand specific competences from workers. In many cases such changes are linked to the introduction of new machinery which itself takes over tasks formerly reliant on the skill and judgement of the worker; the introduction of computer-guided cutting-out in the clothing industry would be an example of this. Formerly such work relied upon the skill of the cutter-out and not in the machines. However, even when skills are in practice made redundant in the labour process, this does not necessarily mean that the workers then come to be regarded as unskilled workers. Their actual job and the technical competences may change, but if the workers and their unions are in a strong enough position then they can retain the status and income of skilled workers even if their actual job has been transformed. It is this latter process, the ability to define jobs as skilled regardless of the technical demands they may have, that feminists have begun to point to as one of the main problems facing women at work, and one which may make it impossible to envisage male and female workers as having the same interests.

Phillips and Taylor have argued that historically the struggle of male workers to defend their own positions, status and income (as well as the important link between forms of work and masculinity itself) has led to a situation where it 'is the sex of those who do the work, rather than its content, which leads to its identification as skilled or unskilled' (Phillips and Taylor, 1980, p. 85) (This overall identification is not to deny that in some cases there will be some basis in the content of work to justify the distinction between male and female, or between skilled and unskilled. But it does at the same time let us see that in many other cases men are claiming skilled status compared to women with all the wage differentials etc. that accompany that position without there being a sufficient difference in the content of their work to justify this distinction. It also points out the way in which work that women do is regarded as unskilled even when it involves a content that is complex. It is not the content that is important: the mere fact that women do such tasks is sufficient to label it as unskilled.) Empirical studies of different occupations are beginning to reveal to us how this situation works out to the disadvantage of women. As Anna Pollert in her study of workers in a tobacco factory comments:

> If job evaluation in general is a mysterious science then the business of judging the value of jobs which (it as happens) are normally done by women must be divinely inspired . . . One might legitimately enquire why a job such as hand stemming (in practice, female) . . . should be rated lower than security patrols? One might hold more responsibility or danger, but the other involves more patience and physical discomfort. Why is a straight-line weigher (in practice, female) . . . in a lower job group than a cigarette-making machine mechanic (in practice, male).   (Pollert, 1981, pp. 66–7).

She points to the way in which the noise and dust experienced by the women workers were not given any points in the grading situation which would have given women a higher total of points in a job evaluation hierarchy, and, in the same way that their conditions of work were ignored so too were their knowledge and skill requirements. The implication is that in such exercises as grading those qualities which women possess are valued so much lower merely because they are possessed by women and that a similar task undertaken by a man would be likely to find itself allocated a much higher grading.

Such situations are not only found in industry: a recent study of white-collar work reached similar conclusions. Crompton and Jones (1984) argue that rewardable or promotable characteristics in the firms they studied (a major bank, a local authority and a life assurance company) were constructed in a manner that systematically excludes women' (Crompton and Jones, 1984, p. 145). As well as this their study led to the conclusion that the qualities that the women did offer were not rewarded. Clerical workers, especially the older women, were not regarded highly yet, for example, in Cohall (the local authority):

> Women in divisional and area offices . . . were often in jobs that required a range of technical and social skills: for example, a part-time clerk-typist had collated, analysed and written up a survey of pre-school provision for children, and a full-time clerk at an adult training centre acted as receptionist/typist/telephonist, compiled the data necessary for accounting purposes, compiled reports and wrote up minutes, invoiced suppliers and kept stockholding records – and, in addition, supervised a mentally handicapped adult trainee for two days a week. (Crompton and Jones, 1984, p. 146)

As they argue it is difficult to avoid the conclusion that had a man been occupying these positions and undertaking these tasks he would soon have been promoted.

In general women do not have the power and positions within unions that would ensure that they and their interests were adequately represented when job evaluation takes place. They and their jobs continue to be devalued with an ensuing lack of promotion and low levels of pay (McNally, 1984). In the meantime men continue to profit, literally, from this situation.

Such arguments about the relationship of technology and skill to male interests are closely related to the question of training. Whilst this state of affairs continues, women will not be regarded as requiring training for their very sex automatically characterises them as 'unskilled'. Such attributes as are technically demanded by their jobs become invisible, they are 'natural' in women. Countries seeking foreign investment for their industrial sector often offer the 'natural' dexterity and docility of their female workers as one of their attractions. Such 'natural' habits have been learned, but in the home and in society not on a training programme. When dexterity is required for men then it becomes an attribute that has to be taught and is part of what makes an occupation skilled. Compositors for newspapers are one example of this, for whilst needing physical strength they also require 'numeracy and literacy, aesthetic sense, dexterity' (Cockburn, 1983, p. 51).

Obviously there will still be some jobs where it is thought that training is required and where women are involved. What is being described here, though, is a more general process, the way in which patterns of thought and behaviour are established. This involves consideration of the processes and structures these are rooted in and which help contribute to the subservient and discriminatory position that women are faced with overall. We are looking at the ideas that women will not need training because they do not do skilled work and that it is skilled work which training is required for. If this approach sets up a general attitude towards women then we can speculate that the identification of a linkage between technology and masculinity, between men and machines will have even more pertinent effects. These will involve training provision and the form in which it should be offered to women. If machinery, whether new or old, is heavily imbued with masculine values and surrounded by a masculine ethos, this points to the value of having all-women workshops and training centres rather than expecting women to somehow 'fit in' with the masculine ethos. Indeed, this is the conclusion reached by many of the voluntary groups involved in training whose ambition it is to open up the forms of work associated with technology to women. It removes women from the atmosphere of resentment and harassment that is often produced by men when women are seen to be entering such 'masculine' occupations. An attitude which is itself a continuation of the attitude those same men will have often displayed to any form of achievment by girls when fellow pupils in the schoolroom. This has, indeed, been one of the reasons why the value of co-educational schooling for women has come under discussion (Deem, 1984; Shaw, 1984). Women need that space in order to develop the confidence and expertise to deal effectively with a masculinised technology and to challenge the gendering of occupations. They need to be able to counter the informal social pressures against women behaving in a way that is necessary for effective functioning in many male-dominated occupations involving machines. For example:

> When you see a woman take a set of spanners and approach a car, you suddenly become aware of the manifold informal pressures against women in public places using their bodies in the way men do: getting dirty and sweaty, climbing up things, lying on the floor, spreading their legs, exerting muscular force. (Cockburn, 1983, p. 19).

Women also have to get away from the pressures that men can exert as co-students:

> There is the pressure of loneliness at work – who do you sit by at tea break. You aren't one of the boys, you can't join in the discussions of sexual conquests and you probably don't want to talk about fishing and football. You can't afford to talk about problems with your boyfriend, it would be ruthlessly used against you. There is the pressure of isolation – what do you do when all the lads are leaning out of the windows whistling at another woman, or discussing a pin-up. There is the pressure on your own sexuality. (Tizard, 1984)

Such pressures are lifted in an all-female training environment, although obviously they can return with full force once a woman is in employment. Until there are more young women in training and the numbers are sufficient to counter such pressure it would seem a priority in training to provide the space in which women can come to terms with technology and traditionally male occupations in a supportive female environment.

CHAPTER 2

Roots

For the first half of this century very little attention was paid to the training of women. In part this reflected the fact that during this period most training was on-the-job training, undertaken in the case of skilled male workers through apprenticeship. The majority of women workers in the pre-second World War period were young and single. The range of jobs open to them was narrow and there was still a predominant belief in all levels of society that a woman's place was in the home. Where employment was undertaken it was in areas seen as synonymous with 'female' interest, in clothing workshops and milliners, in the cotton and cloth trades, or in domestic service. In this situation male defence of skilled jobs did much to reinforce the exclusion of women from other varieties of work, particularly after the First World War. During both World Wars there was the necessity to recruit workers for vital war industries at a time when more and more men were entering the army: this meant that women had to be recruited. Many of these women were drawn from existing industries such as cotton. They moved into engineering and explosives industries, for example, because there was more money and opportunities. However, the period after the First World War also saw the massive re-entry of married women into the workforce. Married women made up 40 per cent of all working women in this period, three or four times the numbers who may have worked previously (Braybon, 1982). This raised fears amongst unions that employers would use female labour to break down their jobs into numerous less skilled areas and threaten hard-won union control over entry to, and content of skilled jobs.

Even in a situation where women were moving into skilled jobs training for them was chaotic in its organisation:

> The recruitment of women for munitions or any other trade was never properly organised: labour exchanges were not fully utilised, women were sent to areas where there was no accomodation available, skilled women were sent to unskilled jobs etc. Nor was there any attempt to standardise training schemes: some firms trained their own workers from the beginning, others took women who had been on government courses at technical colleges and training factories, or to classes set up by private bodies.　　　(Braybon, 1982, p. 101)

In these events we see two themes that were to be repeated over the next fifty years. The first was the unwillingness of the state to intervene in the area of training, whether it involved males or females. The second was the generally limited opportunities open to women, their confinement in the home except in exceptional periods and the fact that any movement away from this situation was perceived as a threat to male jobs by the union movement.

The limits on the state's involvement in the area of training in general reflected the general belief that a state should not intervene too deeply in social matters and especially that it should not intervene in the labour market *per se*. Today we live in a society where the activities of the state are so all-pervading that it is sometimes difficult to realise just how recent a development this is. We now look to the state for regulation in so many areas of our lives that we don't realise that earlier this century the state had many fewer of these policies or responsibilities, and that intervention in the area of training is amongst the most recent of these areas of development, far more recent than intervention in education, housing or health.

In these circumstances it is not surprising that between the First and Second World Wars state activity around training was minimal for everyone. Occasional gestures were made to deal with crises but these were very much exceptional events.

The state set up instructional factories for ex-servicemen after the First World War to deal with that particular one-off problem. With the rapid rise in unemployment in Britain in the 1920s the state again intervened but with temporary programmes aimed at particular groups. When the problem was one of youth unemployment some provision could be made in terms of 'dole schools' or junior unemployment centres which, it has been argued, aimed at 'the prevention of 'demoralisation' and the maintenance of 'employability' through an emphasis on the work ethic' (Rees and Rees, 1982) and which provided girls with the very 'feminine' curriculum of cookery, dressmaking or home nursing. But with youth there was also another alternative on offer, the raising of the school-leaving age which had been set in 1918 at fourteen years of age. Whilst unemployment was very regional in its character, there was also another alternative on offer, that of transference. Schemes were set up to help the unemployed move from areas where demand was depressed to areas where there was a demand for labour. For the girls in such schemes this mainly meant an entry into domestic service:

> It was us in Wales and in different parts like Northumberland. Our mothers were glad (they weren't glad to see us go) for us to go to a meal of food and for someone to clothe us,' cause they wouldn't . . . It was heartbreaking. (A former domestic servant, quoted in Rees and Rees, 1982, p. 25).

The worker was moved to the region rather than the work to the worker in this type of government policy. Even by the Second World War the government response to unemployment and training was minimal and where intervention was countenanced it was again in a need to respond to the hastily mobilised workers being brought into industries to replace those entering the armed forces.

Since the Second World War the situation has been transformed. Today training is a major area of political concern. In the light of rising unemployment both for adults and for young school leavers we have turned to the state for answers, answers related to industrial and economic policy in general. The impact of new technology has made the situation seem one that is even more urgently in need of effective treatment. Very often training is presented as one of the main ways of tackling these problems. However where that training should be sited, whose responsibility it is, how it should be funded and administered and who it should be for, are all questions that receive different answers from different political parties. For what the events of the post-war period have made clear is how much an area like training policy is shaped by political preferences and political ideologies. These relate to the role of the state but above all to the economic policies and theories of the various political parties, for training, like education, (although often dressed in social terms such as equality and opportunity) is very much structured by beliefs as to how the economy should operate and what forces should be involved in it.

In the immediate post-war period and on into the 1950s there was little debate around training opportunities and the main concern of those involved in the area was for apprentices, which by definition then meant a concern for the opportunities of male workers. The number of training centres controlled by the state even fell in this period from 23 in 1951 to 13 in 1962 (House of Commons, 1973b).

The situation in relation to training gradually changed over the following decade and in the 1960s the government began to introduce legislation in the area of training. Since then the involvement of the state in this area has grown considerably so that now it is a major area of government policy and involves considerable financial expenditure. The development of state activity in this area does not, however, necessarily mean that the attitudes of successive governments have always been the same. However, it does mean that governments share a view, albeit from different perspectives, that training is an area of national importance.

In the 1950s and on into the 1960s we can discern different strands of thought and different policy perspectives at play. What they have in common, though, is a continual exclusion of women and their needs as a distinct category in the terms of the debates. Women had been sucked into the labour force in Britain in the Second World War just as they had in the First.

Many of these women were married women who, following
the end of the war, were expected to return to their 'natural'
place in the home and to focus on the rearing of children. The
pressures on women to do this reflected general social ideas on
the role of the women in the home but were reinforced by
other institutional and social structures as well as theoretical
debates. The Welfare State, for example, has developed a
social security system based on a belief in female dependence
within marriage. The infamous 'cohabitation rule' has meant,
for instance, that a woman living with a man can have her
social security payments stopped in the belief that the man
should support her. If he, too, is on social security then he gets
an additional allowance for her but this does not equal the
value of a full single person's allowance.

Pressures and beliefs such as these were reinforced by
theories of 'maternal deprivation', a view which was firmly
propounded by authors such as John Bowlby. His work suggested that even temporary separations from a mother might
be enough to 'scar' a child for life, the mother being the focus of
the deep and vitally important attachment to one person
which each infant had. If this relationship was disrupted, he
argued, then the child could be emotional damaged for the
future and be unable to form stable relationships later in life.
From such a perspective the absence of a mother in paid
employment was potentially threatening to her children. Such
analyses therefore contributed to a general social pressure to
keep married women, particularly those with children, out of
the employed workforce.

Such perspectives also had their effects on the way that both
education and training for girls were envisaged. The need for
any provision in these areas is obviously considered to be
different for those who are expected to withdraw from the
workforce after a short period compared to those whom it is
expected have a lifetime of paid employment before them. In
the 1950s the difference between these two groups seemed
obviously to be that between females and males.

A sub-committee set up under the Ministry of Labour in
1956 produced the Carr Report 'Training for Skill' in 1958.
This report dealt with the adequacy of the training of young

workers for industry and only one short section of it dealt with
opportunities for girls. It was assumed that girls would marry
and that, therefore, they would not need training. Where concern about women was expressed it focused upon the academically above-average grammar school girl who might be
expected to make a more sustained contribution to the labour
force. Similarly in terms of school education the Crowther
Report published in 1959, the year following the Carr Report,
also assumed that the main interest of girls was in their future
roles as wives and mothers whilst recognizing the possibility
that some middle-class girls might combine this with a job. In
1963 the Newsom report also focused on marriage as the main
concern of most girls.

The existence of such beliefs about the role of women and,
in particular, their expression in government reports meant
that existing structures to keep women in this role were reinforced or even further developed. Reports on education, for
instance, were to have effects on the actual curriculum of the
schools. Gender differentiation in subject choice and the
development of clearly feminised or masculinised such as
domestic science and woodwork or metalwork, has been continually isolated in recent analyses as being one of the main
problems in later opening up opportunities for women. Women
lack the qualifications or subject experience that, in many
cases, they need to move into some areas of work. (For an
overview see Stoney, 1984; Deem, 1978.) Such curricular differentiation is only now being challenged, sometimes by the
pupils and parents. These cases are most often concentrated
on those subjects from which pupils find themselves specifically
excluded, such as the exclusion of a girl from metalwork classes
which boys in the same school can take. At other times the main
supporters and prime movers in attempts to limit gender differentiation can be teachers themselves or the LEAs. The fact
remains that, as yet, these efforts are still only patchy and that
a strong differentiation in subjects still exists is illustrated by
examination subjects and results. Whilst this is now being seen
as a cause for concern the result of the education reports of the
1950s and 60s was to reinforce this position because the main
theme of such reports was how to meet the different fields of

interests of male and female pupils, and the differentiation between them was seen as something to be catered for rather than itself transformed.

Against this background it comes as little surprise that when the state started to intervene in the area of training and to issue legislation, the issue of provision for women was not of central importance. For many years Britain, in common with other areas in Western Europe, had continued to feel that the area of training was one that concerned employers and employees rather than the state. The provision of training opportunities had therefore been left to individual firms where it was also a matter of concern to trade unions, especially if it concerned apprenticeship which was used as an entry requirement for skilled work.

However, this process was now considered by the state to be inadequate, especially in the face of overseas industrial competition. The future development of a national industrial base was felt to be at stake and this perspective was linked into more general beliefs about the future direction and development of industry, in particular the growing role of technology and science and assumptions that there was going to be an increasing demand for an ever more skilled and efficient workforce (generally referred to as the 'upskilling' thesis.). From this perspective it was necessary for the state to intervene because employers themselves were failing to provide sufficient training opportunities. Some employers could be considered to be selfish, content to 'poach' workers trained by other firms rather than invest in training themselves. Other firms would react to the poaching by considering training to be a drain on their resources. Firms could be seen as blind to long-term trends and developments, unaware that training was what they would need to run an efficient, cost-effective and challenging business in the future. Whatever the analysis it was sufficient to justify state activity in the area of training, and in 1964 an Industrial Training Bill was brought before Parliament. Industrial Training Boards were set up which were to help establish an overall training policy and oversee its implementation. A levy system on firms would help spread the cost across industry. Yet in the debate around this Bill the problem of training was seen to be one that related only to men, and the absence of women from the debate was publicly noted on occasions (Perry, 1976, p. 106). A belief in the importance of social investment in education and training did not spread to women. An investment has to have calculable returns and to those who made human capital calculations women did not provide such returns, at least in any econom- ically realisable form. Any investment in them could only be made on a more general moral-social basis precisely because of a belief that women would withdraw from the workforce on marriage or with the arrival of children. Any investment in them would therefore be lost. (Woodhall, 1973).

What was also developing in the same period, again to the disadvantage of women when considered in retrospect, was what has been referred to as the 'social democratic repertoire' (CCCS, 1981). Part of this repertoire was the belief in the importance of science and technology, the need for skilled workers and the necessity to reassess Britain's industrial base and its future development. This was all caught up in Harold Wilson's statement that 'The Britain that is going to be forged in the white heat of this revolution will be no place for restrictive practices or for outdated methods on either side of industry' (quoted in CCCS, 1981, p. 97). This economic theme and the stress on a better educated, better trained workforce was then linked into egalitarianism by the Labour Party. However, equality could be expressed in different ways. The most frequent distinction was between equality per se, 'social equality', a society without exploitation, the socialist ideal rooted in fraternity, and, by contrast, the concept of equality of opportunity, the ability of the individual to realise talent. Both elements could be intertwined on occasions and, in the Labour Party, frequently were. Their conjuction was partic- ularly frequent in the area of education and training. CCCS point to this intertwining in Harold Wilson's speeches in the run up to 1964 election:

> I do not want to anticipate the debate on education, but it (the need for scientists) means that as a nation we cannot afford to force segregation on our children at the 11-plus stage. As socialists, as democrats we oppose this system of educational

apartheid, because we believe in equality of opportunity. But
that is not all. We simply cannot as a nation afford to neglect
the educational development of a single boy or girl. We cannot
afford to cut off three quarters or more of our children from
virtually any chance of higher education. The Russians do not,
the Germans do not, the Americans do not, and the Japanese
do not, and we cannot afford to either.

(Harold Wilson, quoted in CCCS, 1981, p. 96).

However, this invocation of inequality revolved around
class and, in particular, reflected the preoccupations of
sociologists of education with social class and educational
opportunity. As such it often involved large-scale quantative
studies. It was class background rather than any other form of
social division that was the main focus of attention. Females
were just part of this overall class category rather than being
regarded as a separate unit of analysis. A commitment to
equality or to equality of opportunity or to both was conceptualised in class terms or, rather, in terms of a unitary class
where gender divisions were unimportant. This was not
unrelated to the fact that many social mobility studies looked
at fathers' occupations and sons' class or status position and
didn't mention women; if women were included it was in relation to their fathers. There is still considerable controversy
over how to conceptualise women in contemporary mobility
studies. Equality, however conceived, was gender-neutral in
rhetoric but inherently male in its application and practice.
Women slipped out of the class category. Equality for all
became, in practice, equality for males. Yet the absence of
women could almost go unnoticed because its slippage out of
the class category was so generally in tune with the more
general social ideologies that believed women's place was in
the home.

Such general social attitudes towards women permeated
discussions around training and its further development.
Unions, employers and the state all reflected and expressed
such attitudes which supported the view that the main place of
women was in the home. This was true even where, as in the
case of the unions, there existed policy documents which
called for equal opportunities for women. The TUC (Trades

Union Congress) had issued a charter for women workers in 1963. In this the need of women workers to receive training was emphasised. In 1972 the TUC was still talking of the need to develop training opportunities for women on the grounds that the impact of the Industrial Training Bill had been negligble for women. The TUC even suggested that forms of positive action should be undertaken to improve the position of women in relation to training. TUC representatives argued that when grants were made to firms from the levy collected across industry the Industrial Training Boards should insist that a proportion of the training places that were set up should be given to women, and that special grants should be given for training for women in 'non traditional' areas, i.e. the occupations dominated by men, as well as for training for those women returning to work after a break from paid employment. Yet at the same time as these calls were being made TUC representatives were also making statements that ran counter to such arguments and, in fact, contradicted these stated TUC goals. For instance, the Expenditure Committee on Employment of women whose sixth report was issued in 1973 noted that:

> The unconscious acceptance of traditional roles and occupations is well illustrated by the TUC evidence which, while favouring equal opportunities for women, describes 'the vast majority of courses' at Government Training Centres as 'clearly appropriate only for men'.

In other words the TUC representatives assumed that certain occupations and therefore the training for them just wasn't open to women. The fact that the majority of the places on such courses were for the engineering and construction industries meant that from this perspective they were 'naturally' unsuitable for women.

This Janus-faced position on the part of the TUC talking of opening opportunities to women with one mouth and denying these for 'natural' reasons with the other clearly relates to the whole question of the masculine ethos of the trade unions. Trade unions can be seen as very much a masculine preserve where men have opposed women's work if it was seen as a threat to their occupations, incomes and privileges, whether these are at work or in the home. Chapter 1 also discussed how the very concept of masculinity had been tied to control over work and the relationship to machinery and technology. From this perspective any expression of interest in opportunities for women becomes seen as little more than a fairly superficial rhetoric and it is therefore unsurprising to find that union representatives saw courses for women as 'unsuitable' because this would have meant entry into arenas where union control was strong and male jobs and wages were jealously guarded.

The state, on the other hand, was not about to oppose such views. With much state legislation supporting the concept of the dependence of women in the home and the 'myth of the male breadwinner', and with the commitment to equality, full employment and economic development conceptualised in an seeningly neutral but actually male manner, it is little wonder that similiar expressions of belief in the true site of women's interests were to be found emanating from members of government departments. The National Council of Women gave evidence to the Expenditure Committee of the House of Commons on the employment of women that:

> a spokesman from the Department of Employment has recently suggested to one of our members that (a) many girls do not want training, (b) the overall employment position should be considered before training more married women; and that (c) it may not be good for the community that married women should be trained, and that the only circumstances in which more women will be trained is when there is economic need.   (House of Commons, 1973)

The effects of these kinds of attitudes could be clearly seen in the figures training. In 1970 only 110 females were apprenticed to the skilled craft occupations compared to 112,000 males, and less than one fifth of those on day release were female. Most women who gaved apprenticeship did so in hairdressing an industry notorious for far pay.

However, if training opportunities for women were limited and if state and unions preferred to cling to the idea that the central focus of women was in the home and with the family and that therefore this was where women should be, this was not what women themselves were either thinking or doing. One of the major features of the expansion of the labour force since the second world war has been the entry of married women into employment. Before the Second World War the female workforce was predominantly young and single; this is no longer the case. Where once women withdrew from the labour force on marriage this no longer necessarily happens and more and more even of those women with young children are going back in to the labour market and seeking paid employment. By 1978 married women made up two-thirds of the total female work force.

This expansion into paid employment has not, of course, meant that women have surrendered their role within the home. They are still looked to as having the major responsibility for house and children and many women will, of course, see their responsibilities this way. Lunch times are often not a break but a chance to dash to the shops, after work becomes a dash home to get the tea and collect the children. This is how women in Angela Coyle's study of female redundancy described their life when they were employed (Coyle, 1984):

> I do as much as I can before I go to work in morning, because I'm so tired when I come home. I go out at lunch time, we only have half an hour and do the shopping. The big shopping I call for on my way home. I tend to prepare meals the night before. Washing I do at the weekends. Big jobs, washing, windows, ironing I do on Sundays. I'm not a religious person.

> When I get up in the morning, I've not much to do because I've done it the night before. I get his shirt and things out, and I do the breakfast things before I go to bed. When I come home from work at the night time, I do an evening meal. If I have some washing I do that then. If it is summer time I peg it out, if not, I put that out the following morning before I go to work. Friday night I go to the late-night opening to do the shopping, my big shop and the rest will be done at the weekend.

Men do very little or where they do help that help tends to be in special areas, the car rather than the ironing, playing with children rather than changing or washing them. Many men, in fact, welcome the changes that are caused if their wives lose their jobs despite the fall in income this mean:

Well, my husband – he wasn't very happy for me because he knew I liked the job and I didn't want to leave, but on the other hand I think he was glad in a way because he thought it was time I stayed at home a bit, he's always been a bit like that.

He likes me at home because he always had to do the dinners, now everything's done for him when he comes home. He was pleased.

(Quoted in Coyle, 1984, p. 42)

This continued responsibility of the women for the home is sustained despite the fact that not only do women go out to work in increasing numbers but that their income is very often a vital element in support of the family. Historically many women have found that they needed to contribute to the family income. In the past this could often take place by work for pay within rather than outside the home, for example by taking lodgers, doing washing, or by small-scale manufacturing especially in the clothing area. Many women still continue to do this piece work within their homes, usually for notoriously low rates of pay, and would not do it unless their financial contribution was valuable. Others work outside the home, often sharing a similarly low rate of pay. Yet even that rate is sufficient to make a major difference to many families that have a male wage coming in, let alone in the families where the woman is the main breadwinner. The number of female breadwinners is rising rapidly; there was a 45 per cent increase in their number in Britain between 1971 and 1978 (to around 725,000), but numerous studies also show that that are many two-income families where it is only the female wage that stops that family falling below the poverty line.

However, if women are entering the workforce in large numbers or staying in the workforce after marriage or even after the birth of their children, this does not mean that they are in an admirable position on the labour market. Many of the women who work after marriage take up part-time work so that they can cope more easily with the demands that are made on them in the home. Many of these part-time jobs are amongst the lowest paid jobs that there are. Often it means that the women are not covered by social security benefits, many employers taking them on for just under the number of hours that would make then eligible for such benefits and which would also involve increased costs on the part of the employer in terms of contributions to the system. The same applies to things like sick leave or holiday pay. There is also some evidence to suggest that in many cases women who go back to work after marriage go back into areas of employment that have lower status and lower pay than the work they did before their work break. For some of these women part-time work has also meant that they were particularly susceptible to being laid off. It has been easier to get rid of them than members of the full-time work force. However, this may depend on the industry or area of work involved, as a recent study of Coventry has shown (Perkins, 1983).

What this massive entry of women into the workforce seems to show is that social ideologies and the lack of positive programmes to encourage women to enter the labour force have not stopped women looking for paid employment outside the home (and the 'offical' figures also hide large numbers of home-workers whose paid work is never accounted for). In 1911 1 in 10 married women had a job; in 1951, 1 in 5; in 1976 1 in 2; and 2 out of 3 employed women are now married (Oakley, 1981, p. 147). For many women this has been done for financial reasons but, as many sociologists like Oakley stress, women also go to work because they like being at work and are bored at home. Being 'an angel at the fireside' is fine in theory but less satisfactory in practice.

More women have also been able to go to work since the Second World War because there have been more jobs for women. With jobs being so clearly sex-labelled in Britain, as in many other countries, expansion, especially in the service sector, has automatically meant an opening up of opportunities for women to work. The fact that it is the service sector that has expanded carries with it an ideology of its own. Services suggest the kind of work that, as one commentator says, is:

> characterised by trim surroundings, neat dress or prestigious uniform, constant exposure to a 'clientele', coffee breaks, telephone calls, culminating, no doubt, in promotion to the Board of Directors or marriage to the boss.   (Kumar, 1978, p. 206)

Yet many of these services do, it fact, exist in a world that is far removed from this idealised picture. Night cleaners, for instance, are just as much part of the service sector as personal secretaries or receptionists. There is also no escaping the fact that when service work is white-collar work much of this can be extremely boiring and tedious. The entry of women into the labour force does not, therefore, open up any glorious world; and the fact that no particular concern or effort was made in the post-war period to open up opportunities for them meant that whilst the characteristics of the female labour force may have changed, the levels at which they worked and the kind of work they were to do was seldom altered.

In the 1970s it looked as though this situation might change. In 1972 and 1973 there were respectively a Green Paper then a White Paper on the question of training, and an Employment and Training Act in 1973 re-ordered the area of training and set up the institution which has become central to any discussion of training today, the Manpower Services Commission. No specific mention of women was made in the Green or White Paper but Section 2 of the Act which enumerated the functions of the Manpower Services Commission made special mention of arrangements that could be made to encourage an increase in the opportunities available to women and girls. Subsequently, as the more detailed discussion in Chapter 4 shows, the Training Services Division of the MSC went on to focus attention on the needs of women in relation to training. In a special report it talked about the inadequate situation in relation to the training needs of women that already existed and the unsatisfied demand amongst women for training opportunities. In this way the report represents the first major initiative and recognition by a state body of the need to do something for women. However, as Chapter 4 shows, there was to be a large gap between acknowledging the problem and actually doing anything concrete about it.

The needs of women were starting to gain public recognition but it is necessary to ask how far this recognition was a cosmetic one, appearing only on the surface. This does not mean that individual members of political parties or of the Manpower Services Commission were not committed to achieving some gains for women in this area; but the attitudes that have been seen to characterise the state, unions, the Civil Service and employers were not going to disappear overnight as their continued existence to the present day only too clearly illustrates.

The commitment made formally by the MSC to developing training opportunities for women took place in the context of other legislation affecting women, the Equal Pay Act and the Sex Discrimination Act. Around this legislation and its operation and impact it is possible to see that state, unions, Civil Service and employers acting in a way to mitigate the effects of the legislation. It is clear by now that women have gained little from the Equal Pay Act as it has been applied in Britain. The terms of the legislation were narrowly drawn, and although pay for women rose initially it has now fallen back to only a little above its original pre-legislation position relative to male wages. Employers have found a number of ways in which to evade equal pay.

Similarly the Sex Discrimination Act (SDA) has proved to be far from satisfactory as far as women are concerned. Part of the problem seems to lie with the Equal Opportunities Commission (EOC) which was set up as the body to administer and oversee the Act. The Commission has been the subject of substantial criticism, the accusation often being made that the Commission as a body (rather than any particular individuals involved in it) has failed to act in an assertive and decisive manner to improve opportunies for women. However, all fault does not lie within the Commission itself. It has been argued that the trade unions have been far from helpful in relation to the EOC because they saw the EOC as a threat. There were fears that, if the Commission were to develop into an active and dynamic body which women could see as representative of their interests this would mean women would turn away from unions as representative of their interests. So far many unions had failed to meet the needs of women workers. Yet unions were beginning to rely on women members as the main source for retaining or increasing membership. Therefore, the unions did not want any competition for membership which might seem to offer a viable alternative. When an individual trade union representative on the Commission tried, on one occasion, to put the interests of the Commission and women first rather than the unions' view, the cost was high because she was not allowed to serve another term on the EOC and was withdrawn from a senior position in the TUC (Meehan, 1983, p. 182)

If the unions were not wholeheartedly behind the SDA neither were some government departments. It has also been argued that the issue of education was an extremely sensitive one and that the Department of Education was very resistant to tackling the issue of sex discrimination in this area:

> The Department of Education and Science has been particularly difficult so far as the EOC is concerned, having been suspicious from the start of proposals for a sex discrimination law. After the passing of legislation, it did little to publicise in its circulars the requirements placed on schools by the Act. Towards the end of 1977 a supposedly confidential report by the Home Office stated that there was no need for an education section in the Commission . . . Dr Byrne of the Commission's Education section was dismissed for discussing the matter with the press, although a tribunal later held her sacking to be unfair. (Meehan, 1983, p. 186)

If unions and the state were involved in resistance to the implications of the Equal Pay Act and the Sex Discrimination Act so too were the employers. One commissioner who was also a member of the Confederation of Britain Industry wrote to the Confederation claiming that it was Confederation representatives who had ensured that the EOC did not have strict codes of practice which employers would have to meet. In the field of legislation specifically dealing with the issues of gender divisions in society and the discrimination experienced by the majority of women it is therefore possible to see the same forces at play that have helped to curtail the specific experiences and opportunities open to women in training. Part of the problem also lies in the fact that legislation for equality has not led to any massive mobilisation of women *per se*. This is unlike other areas of concern which affect women such as abortion (Hoskyns, 1985). Whilst individual women were often very influential in pushing for the legislation the lack of any large scale campaign around sex discrimination must make the task of those resisting it both easier and less public. Essentially, attempts to develop the impact of the legislation have come from two sources, individuals and the EEC.

Many individuals have taken test cases against employers or institutions failing to live up to the terms of the legislation, but there is also pressure from above, from the European Community. Britain legislation has to match the terms of the directives on Equal Pay and Sex Discrimination issued by the Council of the European Communities. If it fails to do so, the government of the day can be challenged for its derogation from the terms of the directive. It is also possible for individual cases to be fought through the national courts and into the Court of the European Communities where the judges can make rulings about the exact implications of the directive and therefore about national legislation which often substantially widen or open up opportunities for women. The Defrenne case, for instance, in Belgium was an early example of how this process could work. Ms Defrenne was a Belgian airhostess who complained about discriminatory practices by her state airline employers and got judgements from the European Court of Justice which upheld her complaints, clarified the EEC policy on Equal Pay and led to a broader policy on women's rights (ROW Europe, 1983).

If this is the overall picture of the general attitudes and atmosphere surrounding equality legislation then it is little wonder that in the area of training no real developments have been made, or made in any noticeable number. If no real commitment existed to transforming the position of women in society, and if representatives of unions, employers and the state could all, on occasions, be identified as actively working against any changes, then it is hardly surprising that such attitudes and opinions have survived relatively unchecked in the area of training. No matter what area related to training we go on to examine, whether it is the Manpower Services Commission, further education, opportunities within work or whatever, the same theme emerges again and again: that women do not have access to the opportunities that would help change the existing pattern of gender segregation in the labour market. Changes require commitment, a commitment that appears largely lacking and which only small numbers of women, often feminists, possess. Such women usually lack access to the resources necessary to change the formal system or present alternatives outside it.

Why have Government, unions and employers as bodies resisted the access of women to training opportunities even when they make verbal and public commitments to their development? One element of the answer must be, of course, the general social attitudes shared by the mostly male members of those institutions. They have been educated, and grown to manhood, in a society which still clings to belief that women only have a secondary role in paid employment and that their primary role is within the home. However, many feminists argue that the question is not just one of attitudes, for attitudes could hopefully be changed. Instead, they point to the material interests of men in having women in this position. Women's secondary role in the labour market keeps the primary one for men: the better jobs, the positions of authority and power, the better levels of pay all go to men who would not willingly lose such privileges. This general position is then made more complex by the different sectional interests of the various groups. Employers have an interest in a flexible, often part-time, poorly paid workforce which in Britain is predominantly female (in other countries it might be made up of migrant labour). Such a workforce helps maintain profit margins. In terms of the state we can see other elements at work. The Thatcher Government certainly is not going to push for equal opportunities when its own political and economic ideology wishes to limit state intervention in all areas of life and give free reign to the market. Political concern too, whatever the government, is always for male not female unemployment which links back once more to those social ideas that the state still expresses, particularly through the social security system, that women are dependent on men. Unions' beliefs about the primary of make exployment are linked to the perception of women as a threat in many areas of work. It is little wonder, then, that wherever we look opportunities for women are so slim.

CHAPTER 3

Contemporary Contexts

So far we have seen that training has been a neglected issue for many years, and that when more resources were diverted into, and state activity began to take effect in this area the end result was a system of training which continued to support gender divisions in the labour market. Today the British labour force is in a state of flux. Major changes are taking place in the composition of the workforce in Britain – some, but not all of which, are related to unemployment. Some occupations are disappearing, the numbers at work are falling, but geographically the labour force is also changing. Some old basic industries are in decline, such as shipbuilding and coal mining, others such as clothing are moving their factories into new areas. Some of the new jobs that are being created, especially in the area of new technology are clustering together in the south-east. Changes such as these obviously affect women for they alter the labour market that women enter. They also affect women in other ways for the question of whether women work or not, especially married women, is often related to levels of male employment. Where male unemployment is high, it may not be worth loss of benefit for wives of unemployed men to be in low-paid employment.

This regional restructuring and recomposition of the workforce is one element to consider in assessing the current impact of training opportunities for women and how these may need to be shaped for the future. Another vital element in the equation is new technology. New technology is not just producing some new forms of jobs that we haven't had before, it is also affecting present occupations, reshaping them, producing new forms of hierarchy and new possibilities for promotion as well as new limitations. In considering the question of training we therefore also need to take this new technology dimension into consideration. A further factor also has to be taken into consideration when discussing training for women: race. It is already clear that women from different class backgrounds and at different ages are likely to approach the problem of employment differently. The pressures on a woman from a middle-class home to provide a steady income for her family are unlikely to be as strong as those from a working-class background; the former could perhaps afford to be fussier about the kind of work they do or wait longer to find the kind of employment they want. Women from middle-class homes are also likely to have stayed at school longer and to have more and better qualifications which give them access to a wider variety of more interesting and possibly better paid jobs. Women whose children are grown up or are teenagers are going to find going out to work easier than women struggling with toddlers and small children who have to fit in childminders and school hours. However, even when these differences between women are recognised the issue of race adds a further dimension to the argument. Women from ethnic minority groups may well have different employment patterns, (sometimes these are strong cultural barriers to their being employed at all); they also tend to be strongly clustered in particular areas which can also affect their employment opportunities. The children of ethnic minority groups may have different educational experiences, different reactions and aspirations to those of their parents but black teenagers, for example, may still be distinguishable from white youth in this respect. If training is to make a satisfactory contribution to their needs then these differences have to be acknowledged and catered for, and the problem of the institutionalised racism invested in many public institutions including training organisations should be both confronted and countered. All these problems, the changing composition and geographical location of the labour force, the impact of new technology and the different responses and opportunities available to ethnic groups, have to be kept in mind when assessing the present structure and impact of existing training opportunities for women.

The first of these factors, the restructuring and relocation of the labour force, is perhaps the most invisible, a case of not seeing the wood for the trees. We all know the problems of rising unemployment, the familiar head-count of jobs lost and jobs gained at the end of television news bulletins. At a more personal level we know the problems faced by those made redundant, friends and relatives who've lost their jobs, the sudden redundancies or the lack of any job at all for many young school leavers, including our own children. Yet these personal experiences seldom gell together into an overall pattern other than the simple one of unemployment. News bulletins add and subtract jobs but they don't explain the implications of the changes, not do we get an overall view of them. Yet Doreen Massey has argued that it is urgent to recognise the extent and depth of the changes that are occurring in Britain today (Massey, 1983). She has argued that there is a process of industrial decline affecting both specific regions and specific occupations, and that the employment that remains is being restructured geographically; the sites of employment are changing and 'the decline of the old is not always happening in the same place as the rise of the new' (Massey, 1984, p. 25). Even old jobs that aren't disappearing, industries that aren't going under, are often relocating their factories and production lines in new areas of the country. It is not the aggregate situation that is so important, the overall numbers of jobs gained and lost, as much as where work is disappearing, where work is coming, what kind of work is left or being created and who is getting these jobs.

For women, who as we have seen, are making up an increasing percentage of the labour market, these changes are very important. This points to the necessity of taking local labour markets into consideration when working out how to develop training opportunities rather than just relying on a picture of the country as a whole. Local opportunities are essential but the question of jobs open to women has to be related to the work opportunities available for men. In areas where the dominant form of employment for men means a lot of shiftwork or involves very long hours then married women, especially those with children, will be limited in the kinds of work that they can take on. For example, Doreen Massey in her discussion of coal mining regions says:

> As far as paid employment is concerned, the opportunities for women have been extremely limited in these regions throughout the century. This has been related to the nature of employment for men and the status attached to it. The demands put on (female) domestic labour by male work down the mine are enormous. Shiftwork, too, makes it more difficult for both partners to be employed outside the home. The ideology of a sexual division of labour between breadwinner and homekeeper has probably become more firmly entrenched in these areas than anywhere else in the country.
>
> (Massey, 1983, p. 25)

Thus we can see that not only do some male occupations make it difficult for women in areas where those occupations predominate to go out to work, but that jobs also set up expectations about what men and women ought to do, especially in the home. These expectations then easily become traditions. We see whole areas where the community does not expect married women or women with children to work outside the home, and these traditions then keep women within the home even when the labour market in such regions changes and there are opportunities for paid employment for women (Gale and Marks, 1974). Such pressures are an important consideration for it is precisely in many of the areas where men have worked in occupations such as mining, steelmaking and shipbuilding that the decline in male employment is the greatest. Yet if women have not been accustomed to going out to work, if their mothers, sisters and friends have stayed at home with their children then they will be under social pressure not to work. They will not have the access to jobs or expectations of work that might make transition into paid employment that much easier. In this situation the importance of the provision of return to work courses cannot be underestimated. Nor can the special needs of women be neglected. A strong division of labour in the home does not always break down with unemployment of the men. They might be at home all day but this doesn't mean that they are necessarily prepared to share the housework or childcare – or even that many women would want them to. Yet if the women are to have opportunities to prepare for work they will need training courses which allow for the problems of childcare either by fitting in with school hours and holidays or by providing childcare facilities at the training site.

If jobs are disappearing in some regions other industrial sectors and other occupations are also being relocated. In many instances this process means that more jobs for women become available in these new locations. Our child benefits are administered from Newcastle, for instance, we get new driving licences and car ownership details from Swansea. Both of these everyday facts represent elements in a process of decentralisation in Britain today. Both benefits and car registration are aspects of government administration but instead of being sited near the heart of government in London they are to be found out in the regions and offering many women there the chance of employment.

Other forms of regional change in employment which affect women are also occurring. Changes in the technology of production have given many firms the opportunity to move site. This is especially true in industries such as telecommunications, electrical engineering and electronics. The changes within Britain echo developments that are taking place on a world scale with production being moved to take advantage of groups of workers. Within the UK manufacturing which has moved has often moved precisely to catch new groups of workers for its production processes. In many cases these new workers are women, very often older, married women. Workers like these are often called 'green labour' as they sometimes lack previous experience in the jobs, and tend not to have had trade union experience. They are therefore often considered by employers to be a more malleable source of labour than men and women with a longer and more traditional industrial background. The move is also often to more isolated areas of the country or to smaller towns or housing estates where job opportunities are fewer and therefore the workforce is presumed to be less likely to cause trouble, because loss of work will be permanent if no other openings are available in the vicinity. Employers are also thought to favour the seeking out of new groups of female workers where technology and the labour process make this possible, because they offer a source of cheap labour. Despite the operation of the Equal Pay Act women's wages still remain substantially lower than men's (around 71 per cent (EOC, 1981)). If the fact that many women are employed part-time is taken into consideratiqn then the savings to many employers are even greater than a mere wage comparison would suggest because women can be employed to just under the limit where social insurance had to be paid by the employer.

Some of the jobs that are being created in new areas are therefore not the most desirable for women in terms of levels of pay and opportunities for promotion and development. However, for many women they offer an eagerly awaited opportunity for employment which training schemes have to acknowledge and cater for. Realistic assessment and an introduction to employment possibilities must form an important element in 'Return to Work' courses.

If many of the 'new' jobs that are appearing in the regions offer women no better prospects than those they have always experienced – other than that of employment per se, – the advent of new technology could alter this situation. New technology brings with it occupations that no longer require physical strength in any way, indeed they often draw upon precisely those characteristics such as dexterity that have been associated with women. Cynthia Cockburn in her study of technological innovation amongst compositors in the newspaper industry describes the sense of shock that is experienced at first seeing men crouched over the keyboards of VDUs (visual display units):

> To our eyes, used to seeing women and girls sitting at typewriters, the men in their shirt-sleeves, often quite heavily built men used to more strenuous manual work, do indeed seem out of scale with the new equipment   (Cockburn, 1983, p. 96)

Very often the introduction of new technology is considered to be a fundamentally benign process, part of a march of progress towards the development of an 'information society', the coming of a new golden age. Associated with such views are a general view of such a future as involving better work and living conditions for all, greater participation in society through interactive machines in the home, with easy access to banking, shopping and entertainment facilities. In such an analysis the process of transition to such a new form of society is bound to involve casualties, people will lose jobs in much the same way that handloom weavers and spinners working in their homes lost work in the face of the growth of factories during the Industrial Revolution. The problem then is seen as one of mitigating such effects and this is the position that many unions in Britain have taken in relation to the introduction of new technology (Robins and Webster, 1982). This adaptive and defensive posture has led to an emphasis on the importance of consultation and retraining during the introduction of new technology, but essentialy unions have regarded the advent of technological changes as something that has to be gone along with if they and their members are to survive and prosper. Such views are not, however, always shared by those on the shopfloor:

'I don't look on new technology as progress,' a compositor said. 'You have to ask, is it conducive to a better society or a better atmosphere? The way they are introducing it, it is not. They are taking no account of people'.

(Robins & Webster, 1982)

In the majority of cases it is women who are having to bear the brunt of the impact of new technology. It is generally agreed that office work is one of the areas most likely to be transformed in the first wave of new technology. Sectors such as banking and insurance are already undergoing major changes, for example banking is now dealing with the electronic storage and transfer of information and funds. Clerical work in general will also be transformed with the introduction of wordprocessors (as indeed is the production of this book), whether the office concerned is that of a small country solicitor or the massive edifice of a multinational. Even the areas of manufacturing and retailing will not be exempt. Office work which is very labour intensive offers a prime site for the introduction of new machines, and with them new ways of working. It offers employers the possibility of improved productivity and holds out the hope of cost-cutting (West, 1982). At least part of this cost-cutting lies in the possibility that fewer people will be needed to do the same amount of work. Examples abound of the ways in which the introduction of new technology has resulted in job losses. In one case the preparation and checking of football pools which had previously occupied 130 part-time workers for 7 to 15 hours could be done by 2 people in 3½ hours using a computer (Leeds, 1982, p. 5). However, this need not necessarily always be the case. If business develops sufficiently quickly the employment figures can remain static, with the result that the same number of people could now be handling increased business, and there could even be the possibilities of some small rises in employment (West, 1982).

As women make up the majority of office workers they are obviously those most likely to be affected by these developments. In the UK one-third of women work in offices, 90 per cent of these in routine jobs such as clerical work and typing. All of these women are susceptible to the impact of new technology. If jobs in these areas go, or and the very least there is a curtailment in the growth of office jobs, many women will find their return to work increasingly difficult because the job opportunities are no longer there. In other cases women will find their traditional skills such as speed typing outdated, and it has been suggested that older workers in particular will find it hard to adjust to changes (Werneke, 1983, p. 33).

Such developments obviously have implications for the provision of training facilities. Women need the opportunity to become acquainted with the new technology of the 'electronic office', the wordprocessors, facsimile machines, microcomputers etc. Nor is it just a question of catering for those who feel out of touch after a break from paid employment. Many young school leavers will not have had the opportunity in school to become familiar with such equipment either.

However, there still remain other problems associated with the introduction of new technology which will adversely affect the position of women in the world of work, and these are less simply dealt with by the provision of training facilities. The introduction of new technology is also associated with increased control. Indeed, some argue that wordprocessors, for instance, 'are specifically designed for increased management control over the labour process as well as directly raising productivity,' (West, 1982, p. 72).

> Tuesday 10.30 p.m.: the lone computer operator comes over to my console and says in a friendly way 'If you're going to stay here, you'll have to get your productivity up'
>
> 'Oh,' I say, 'What is my speed and what should it be?'
>
> 'It's been scientifically set', he tells me 'at 50,000 keystrokes an hour'.
>
> Then he sits down, plays a couple of chords on his control panel and up come my figures. The figures show when I started – to the nearest tenth of a second – when I took a break and exactly how many keystrokes I'd done all evening . . . the real supervisor is inside the machine.
>
> (Mosco, 1982, p. 119).

With such developments the nature of control in the office becomes clearer; it is not longer hidden by personal relationships with bosses or supervisors. Women also lose what little autonomy they had, the management of their own time and space in the organisation of their working day (West, 1982; Downing, 1980).

However, increased control in the office, the speed-up of work and increased stress are not the only unfavourable outcomes for women as the result of the introduction of new technology. A change in job content and work organisation often goes hand in hand with the use of new technology. Reports from North America and Europe suggest that a new hierarchy is being introduced into the office; that we will see the development of a group of lower-level skilled clerical workers, many of whose current skills such as layout and shorthand will become redundant. These workers will do increasingly simplified forms of work as the machines take many tasks from them (although this is not to suggest that office work *per se* is generally a highly skilled and satisfactory occupation: studies of office workers nearly always find that women would value more autonomy in their work even in a situation where new technology has not yet been introduced).

Above them will emerge a group of workers who become more concerned with administration – although it is unclear whether this separate level will have any increased access to job opportunities or a career ladder. Some writers suggest that these women too could find themselves segregated together in administration centres and would not be considered likely candidates for promotion (West, 1982). On other occasions it seems to be suggested that this second level will be required to have a much wider area of knowledge than existing secretaries and will require a better understanding of administration, office procedures and the use of word- and data-processing. In many cases it is likely that there will be a complete discontinuity between this level and the lower level. Women who might have once moved up and out of the typing pool may well find themselves permanently segregated. Access to the higher levels will be from the outside, from those coming in with the qualifications required. To break down such distinctions would require the development of different forms of work organisation than now seem to be occurring; but if such changes continue it seems that forms of training will have to be provided to give at least some women access to such positions. Whilst the change will have to start in the schools, and women's analytical capabilities encouraged and developed, it is also likely that post-school training should be changing. A report from the ILO has suggested that more than just replacing typing classes with instruction in wordprocessing is required:

> the concept of training must move from providing task-specific skills to giving a broader understanding of an organisation as a system and must lay the basis for continuous retraining over a career.   (Werneke, 1983, p. 98)

It seems, therefore, that even with this pessimistic interpretation of the impact of new technology, training will have an important role to play. The same is true of other areas besides office work. Health care is another area where employment for women is important and which is also being affected by new technology:

> With the exception of the medical laboratory technicians and remedial gymnasts, health care is predominantly female. Today about 90 per cent of physiotherapists are women, though men concentrate their activities in the teaching and superintendent posts. The implications of computer technology are beyond doubt very great. Throughout the West Midlands Regional Health Authority computer technology is being applied in a variety of services such as blood transfusion, radiation protection and treatment of visually, mentally and physically handicapped.   (Sharp, 1984).

On the other hand there is also the question of the creation of new jobs through the development and spread of microtechnology. Again it is hard to future-gaze, but certain occupations have already been pinpointed as growth areas. These include computer applications – programming, systems analysis, data management and electronics engineering (Werneke, 1983, p. 34). Yet if the present situation continues the outlook for women does not appear to be rosy. Many of these 'new' occupations are graduate ones and the number of women who can enter these occupations is limited by their educational experience. Very few women are in the engineering, maths and science faculties of higher education which would give them the necessary qualifications and, of course, this links back once again to the problem of school experiences. However, not all jobs require degrees and it is not impossible for women to be given compensatory training when they are starting to prepare for such employment. That such a development is not impossible is shown by the activities of the South Glamorgan Training Workshop which has set up just such a introduction to its programmes aimed at women wishing to enter the field of microelectronics. Such a provision is doubly important when it is linked with the fact that it is precisely those sectors using new technology, whether in offices or in production, that find it most easy to locate in the 'green fields' of the regions. New technology makes the process of decentralisation of work in Britain that much easier.

It is clear that massive changes are taking place in the location of job opportunities and that both the destruction and creation of new employment opportunities can also be structured by the development and impact of new technology. However, these changes do not affect all women equally. Class and age differences affect the entry of women into employment and in contemporary Britain ethnic minority groups membership is also a powerful influence on education, employment and 'training experiences for many women. Membership of ethnic minority groups may differentiate between those who otherwise may be members of the same sex and the same class; thus is particularly the case for black women.

The question of black women is particularly important because there we find women who are the objects of double discrimination: they are discriminated against in the labour market because they are women but also discriminated against because they are black. The jobs that women can get are defined in terms of femininity and this femininity is culturally specific.

> Griffen cites an example of a woman administrator, working in local further education provision, who engaged a young Afro-Caribbean woman as secretary and who had purposely practised 'positive discrimination' because of young black women's doubly disadvantaged position in the local labour market. She had been astounded at the reactions of her white colleagues and visitors. On hearing 'Yvonne' answer the phone, or seeing her in the office, visitors would assume that she was the cleaner – simply due to the race-specific and racist assumptions about young black women's position in employment
> (Parmar, 1982).

Despite attempts to deny it, racism is now strongly ingrained in British Society (Swann Report, 1985). The anecdote above goes some way to illustrating the kinds of assumptions that structure the experience of ethnic groups in the labour market. Whether those concerned are immigrants or whether they are the British descendents of immigrants they tend to be harder hit by unemployment (Cross, 1982; Dex, 1983). For instance, it is estimated that two young West Indians are unemployed for every single 'indigenous' youngster that is unemployed. For women in the ethnic groups the situation is even worse. Females seem to be more affected by unemployment than males. In 1975, for example, the rate of increase in unemployment for black male workers was twice as large as the general increase in employment, but for black women workers the increase was three times as large.

The fact that racism and discrimination on grounds of race exists in Britain is a general one, but even within this situation the impact on women from different ethnic groups is not always the same. Many elements enter into this new differentiation. The overall discrimination practised in society is one element, but there are also differences among the female members of these groups, between Asians and Afro-Caribbean or Cypriot women, for example. On the other hand there can be a joining up of members of different ethnic groups on the basis of religion, for example, and they can form a social and work network (Khan, 1979) which is important to the female members. Members of these different groups often have different employment participation rates, especially amongst first-generation immigrants. This situation is then further complicated by whether these women have children of not. Afro-Caribbean women have a participation rate in employment that is far higher than that of the general population (Cross, 1978; Moss, 1981). Muslim Asian females, on the other hand appear far less likely to be in paid employment, especially those from Pakistan. Numerous explanations are put forward to try and explain these differences in employment participation rates. In the case of Afro-Caribbean women, for example, the suggestion has been made that female migration to Britain and their high employment rates can be linked to cultural factors:

> Prescod- Roberts, explicitly linking education with future earning power, suggests why girls in the West Indies may be supported by their family to pursue educational qualification. In a migratory economy decisions have to be made as to who will reliably send remittances once they have migrated. She suggests that the sexual division of labour and responsibility within the family locks women more strongly and permanently into family responsibilities than it does men, and so makes women the better migrants from the perspective of those left behind. (Fuller, 1982)

These immigrants then have a higher participation rate because they are working for those at home in the West Indies as well as themselves in Britain. Mary Fuller, in fact, questions whether such an explanation is necessary and points to the realities of racial and sexual exclusion in Britain as accounting for Afro-Caribbean women's search for qualifications and work. The low pay and poor employment prospects for the majority of black male workers make a female wage a necessity for many black households in Britain. Numerous studies have shown that Asian women are also subject to similar economic pressures, 'high mortgage repayments, high rents and the increasing cost of living' are the reasons most frequently given by Asian women workers. (Parmar, 1982, p. 247).

Women from ethnic minority groups are also faced with assumptions about them as women and about their social and familial relationships that also help structure and determine the opportunities open to them. Fears have been expressed, for instance, about the effect of Asian women working in paid employment on the assumption that 'normal' cultural patterns meant women did not do such work. But as Parmar points out the majority of these women come from societies where they will work extremely hard inside and outside the home, what is new is that they have not worked in an industrial situation before (Parmar, 1982). Assumptions about strongly patriarchal Asian families and a belief that young Asian women will rapidly disappear into wifehood and motherhood structure the opportunities they are given even more than for most women. In the youth training schemes run by the Manpower Services Commission precisely such features have occurred:

> The prevalence of sex role stereotyping existing in the wider context of society is reflected in YOP schemes through gender-appropriate training courses such as community service, sewing and typing for the young female trainees and building maintenance, carpentry and painting and decorating for the young male trainees. This gender-ascribed job training is compounded by specific cultural and racial features in the case of Asian girls. One YOP scheme in Yorkshire trained the predominantly Muslim female trainees by taking them out to the

park for walks and their work placement consisted of them
watching male trainees dig up old peoples gardens.

(Quoted in Carby, 1982, p. 204)

For many women of ethnic groups the situation for employment is also regulated very strongly by regionalism and by the
structure of local labour markets. Whilst culture and religion
may be an important explanatory variable in shaping the
experiences of women in the different ethnic groups, the structural constraints they face must also be considered and whilst
this is obviously a problem faced by all workers it is especially
severe for members of ethnic groups because there is an
uneven pattern of ethnic group settlement. Blacks are especially clustered in the Greater London area, the West Midlands
and West Yorkshire. According to the areas, job opportunities
can vary even for the same ethnic minority group. Afro-
Caribbean women in London are found mainly in service
occupations, for instance, but in the West Midlands they are
largely found in engineering occupations. The opportunities
that are available to women will therefore depend on the occupations and sectors that are open to them and the extent to
which these have survived or closed in the recent recessionary
period.

For black women who are mothers childcare can be a
problem that structures their employment possibilities. They
may only seek part-time or home work in order to cope with
the demands made by small children, just as white women do.
While there may be relatives or other older women who will
undertake childminding, many must rely on paid childminders
and this is an area where there are accusations of racism, with
the concurrent disadvantages for black workers. A summary
of a study on working mothers and childminding says:

First, black women are less able to get access to day care
provision they most desired than were white mothers. Second
they had less access to subsidised or free services, i.e. day
nurseries and nursery schools. Third, they had greater difficulty finding childminders near their home. And finally, some
white minders refused to take black children. All these point to
the force of racism in conditioning the lives of black women.

(Parmar, 1982, p. 248)

These three elements – race, region and technology – all contribute to a picture which is deeply complex. All of them obviously deeply affect training for women because they will all have to be taken into account in assessing the level and type of training provision to be made. What is the local labour market like for women? What has it traditionally been like? Which occupations are in decline, which are developing? What kind of community is it? What are the requirements of the different groups in the community? Have there been particular problems in relation to schooling etc. that will need dealing with? All these and other questions would need to be faced in the pursuit of relevant training opportunities. The answers to such questions need to underpin any response in training terms.

However, whilst recognising this on-the-ground complexity it is also the case that more general themes in relation to training can be picked out. Areas like the provision by the MSC, in further education colleges, in industry and on the job, can be categorised together on a national basis because there are general weaknesses in them all in relation to the provision that is made for women. After analysis general suggestions can be made as to the type of actions that can be undertaken to improve women's opportunities, but the analysis and discussion of these general problems must always be undertaken with the knowledge that general changes will not in themselves be enough and that there are much more local needs which have to be taken into account.

CHAPTER 4

Youth Training Programmes

In 1973 an Employment and Training Act was passed which provided for the setting up of the Manpower Services Commission. Since that time the Commission has developed enormously in status and power. Today it is active not just in government training centres but in further education, in schools, in community projects, in a myriad of places, which makes it one of the most influential institutions in Britain today. Its activities have helped to bring training into the spotlight and have made the provision of training a central political issue.

The rise and rise of the MSC is not something that has taken place in isolation; rather it is part of a wider swing towards a new vocationalism that it is also affecting schooling and which has taken place in the context of rising unemployment, particularly youth unemployment. The new vocationalism has found its impetus in a belief that education and schools could be partly held responsible for the fact that many young people are failing to find employment. This analysis emerged during the Great Debate around education which took place in the mid-1970's. School leavers were thought not to be getting jobs because individual pupils in the schools were failing to get the skills that they required and the kind of experiences that were necessary if they were to be successful on the labour market. A finger of blame was then pointed at the schools whose curricula and teaching methods were assumed to be at fault if numerous young people were leaving the schoolroom unprepared for the competition of the labour market. While the recession was not yet at its height it was easier to conceptualise the problem as one of lack of skills and experience in individuals. This point of view has been maintained despite the worsening of the recession and the obvious signs that some young people are never going to get jobs, not because they lack the attributes that work requires, but because the work just isn't there.

However, the initial focus on the inadequacies of particular youngsters certainly helped in the rise of the MSC. This became an institution under whose aegis remedial programmes could be set up to to help counter the failings of the educational system. Much of the subsequent growth of the MSC has come in this area of work, yet the MSC was not set up with precisely this work in mind. The youth programmes developed out of the Holland Report of 1977, 'Young People at Work' (MSC, 1977), but the MSC itself had been in existence since 1974. The MSC had two executive arms, the Employment Services Division and the Training Services Division. The Training Services Division was to be responsible for TOPS (the Training Opportunities Scheme) which was to replace old vocational schemes in government Training Centres. Furthermore the Act which set up the MSC and enumerated the functions of the Commission made special mention of arrangements that could be made to open up training opportunities to women and girls.

In 1976 the Training Services Division brought out a report on 'Training Opportunities for Women' (MSC, 1976). This followed a decision in 1975, the year of the Equal Pay and Sex Discrimination Acts, that the training needs of women should be treated as a special priority for the Commission. The Sex Discrimination Act had, in fact, tried to encourage the opening up of training opportunities for women by exempting certain forms of training provision from the terms of the Act. Section 47 allowed for positive discrimination in the provision of single-sex training courses where men or women were training for jobs in which the number of people of their sex was extremely small in the previous year. It also allowed for schemes in particular areas. Section 47 also recognised the problems of those returning to work after a period of domestic responsibility (almost always women) and permitted both special training schemes and discrimination in the selection for training programmes for those in this category.

The MSC report on training opportunities for women acknowledged that there was an unsatisfied demand for training from women and that there were economic, social and legislative justifications to provide them with training. It also recognised that the training provision that was currently being made was inadequate in every area, whether it concerned day release and apprenticeships or government training schemes.

This recognition of the problems faced by girls and women in getting access to training and the formal commitment to changing the situation was to be echoed in the areas of the MSC that dealt with adults, such as the TOPS courses, and was also evident in relation to the schemes set up to cope with the problems assumed to be facing young school leavers. The Holland Report on young people led to the establishment of a third section inside the MSC, the Special Programmes Division, which emerged in 1978. The committee responsible for the report had concluded then that youth unemployment could be expected to rise as a result of demographic trends until at least 1981, but as was to become rapidly clearer the problem of unemployment was to be more than a mere demographic one. Existing schemes to cope with the problem were regarded as piecemeal and *ad hoc* and were distributed amongst a number of uncoordinated agencies. The Special Programmes division was to attempt to transform this situation by offering a coherent programme for the young unemployed.

Although the number of young people unemployed was already rising rapidly and was starting to be a matter for general concern throughout the European Community and not just in Britain, it was still possible at this time to conceptualise the problem as one of a mismatch between the individuals seeking jobs and the opportunities available in the labour market. The problem was conceptualised as one that was rooted in the individual who had failed to acquire rudimentary skills during schooling and therefore the special programmes could be seen as precisely that, a special effort to deal with inadequacies in a few individuals with whom the schools had failed to cope. And while there were, at the same time, pressures on the schools to transform their curricula and to ensure basic literacy and numeracy in a core curriculum, the special programmes could be seen as repairing the damage. The MSC's activities in the area of youth unemployment therefore started as a short term intervention in what was regarded as an area of concern for only a few individuals, rather than youth in general. This situation has changed as the problem of youth unemployment has increased and as the duration of unemployment has lengthened. Analyses now suggest that we are seeing a whole generation, many of whom will never have any opportunity to enter paid work. As a result MSC programmes for youth are now oriented towards more permanent activities to cater for this generation and such concepts lie behind more recent developments such as the New Training Initiative which led to the setting up of the Youth Training Scheme (YTS).

However, the first courses and programmes were set up with this view of the problem as a more temporary phenomenon and with their establishment it seemed possible that training opportunities for female school leavers would improve. The establishment of the debate as one concerning 'youth' opened up the possibility that schemes would cater for females as well as males and the MSC's stated interest in opening up opportunities for women offered ground for optimism.

The Youth Opportunities Programme that was set up (YOP) offered work experience schemes and work preparation courses. Both these elements were thought to offer young people access to the kind of skills and opportunities that they had failed to find during their period of schooling.

In the first year, 1978/9, there were 162,200 participants in the scheme (MSC Annual Report, 1978/9). By 1981/2 over 500,000 were taking part. This represented a rise from 1 in 10 school leavers to 1 in 2, a trend that has subsequently continued and which has meant that for many school leavers MSC programmes offer the nearest they are ever going to get to the world of paid employment. Within the YOP scheme the position of women seemed excellent on the surface. Female school leavers made up around 50 per cent of those participating in the YOPs and they maintained this percentage despite the rise in absolute numbers. However, once the actual pattern of experience is analysed a different picture begins to emerge and this was one that clashed with the MSC's own stated commitment to female opportunities.

In 1979 a report was published on the opportunities available to women in the special programmes of the MSC. A central theme in the report was the entry of women into 'masculinised' or 'non-traditional' areas of work. The report recognised that 'there are practically no jobs which cannot be done by girls, given the opportunity and appropriate training' (MSC, 1979). It also admitted that the female workforce suffered from specific forms of disadvantage, including the problem of lack of confidence. The question of educational qualifications was also raised, especially the failure of many women to acquire the kind of mathematical and technical qualifications that were required for entry into training in some areas of employment. The problems of older women with domestic responsibilities was also acknowledged. The report stressed the importance of not reinforcing existing sexual stereotypes in relation to work and the fact that courses, work experience schemes and temporary schemes should try to avoid this and in doing so make use of the exemptions allowed by the Sex Discrimination Act.

However, it soon became clear that the commitments of this report were to remain more or less at the level of rhetoric. Work experience schemes always made up the majority of places on offer under the YOP programme, offering around 462,000 places in 1981/2 compared to 92,000 places on the work preperation courses. The majority of these work-experience places, roughly constant at around 80 per cent, were with private employers and tended to be concentrated in small, low paying and non-unionised workplaces (Youthaid, 1981). The whole Youth Opportunities Programme very soon came in for substantial criticism, criticism that even the MSC was, in the end, to admit had some foundation. Complaints were made that the MSC did not have the resources to evaluate or monitor the placements that were set up and that abuses of the system by employers were widespread. In some cases the complaints were focused on job substitution. Employers were accused of taking on work – experience placements and using the young people to do the work that should have been done by full-time employees. In this way the employers were availing themselves of a source of cheap labour that a government institution was making available to them. The end result was a situation in which many jobs were destroyed; indeed it has been speculated that YOP actually destroyed more jobs than the recession did (Finn, 1983). YOP openings began to be treated as normal job vacancies (EMCO, 1982) with no security for the workers but with the advantage of cheap labour for the employers. Little wonder then that unions and Trades Councils, many of whom had welcomed initiatives that would attempt to deal with the employment problems of young people, were becoming alarmed about the role of the Youth Opportunities Programme and union participation and co-operation with the scheme (Sheffield Trades Council, 1982). Numerous accidents and some deaths also occurred on the schemes, mainly due to what was thought to be inadequate safety provisions and safeguards (2,615, accidents, 32 amputations and 5 deaths in 1981–2 – quoted in Finn, 1983). It seemed that the Youth Opportunities Programme was rapidly transforming itself into a temporary work programme and not a programme of preparation and development.

For female entrants into the YOP schemes the picture was even bleaker for not only were they caught up in a scheme whose general inadequacies soon began to become apparent; they also found themselves in a scheme which served to help reproduce and perpetuate the gender stereotyping about employment and occupations which already existed. The opportunities that the female entrants were being offered were firmly circumscribed and reflected only the limited job opportunities open to women. They did not really come to terms with the problems that the MSC had itself identified as affecting women in the report on training opportunities for girls in the special programmes. National surveys of participants in YOP which were undertaken for the MSC consistently revealed the gender stereotyping at work. There was gender stereotyping evident in the parts of the YOP programme that males and females entered and there were also significant differences within those parts. There were far more males than females in the project-based work experience sectors and in the training workshops. Female entrants, on the other hand, dominated the community service sector. Oviously the dominance of the female entrants in the community sector reflected general imagery of women as the 'carers', whilst even within the training workshops and project based schemes the small proportion of female entrants were likely to find themselves confined to activities that were seen by entrants and managers and staff as 'female'. In the work experience on employers' premises and in the short training courses the proportion of male and female entrants was far more equal, yet once again there was further reinforcement of occupational segregation by sex. A study in Fife, for example, found that 80.5 per cent of boys had their YOP experiences in the industrial manufacturing sector whilst 81.5 per cent of the girls were to be found in the service sector (Brelsford, 1983). In fact, it is possible to argue that YOP led to a narrowing of opportunities for female entrants and actually shut off options in an already narrowly segregated female labour market. Figures show that before joining YOP 68 per cent of girls who had had a job were in clerical, selling, catering and personal service work (the 'female' occupations), and that after YOP this proportion rose to 74 per cent (Rees, 1984). In areas like Northern Ireland where there is an even narrower range of occupations available to women and where the unemployment rate is higher than in most other areas of Britain the opportunities open to women appear to have been even further restricted. Women were commonly to be found on the cheaper schemes and in the courses for the less able whilst the men dominated the schemes which offered recognised training. Much of the traditionally female work on offer through the programme such as textiles and sewing seemed unlikely to offer much hope for the future for these industries are in rapid decline. Where they do survive they seem to show a preference for part-time, married, experienced workers (Rees, 1983).

It seems clear, therefore, that although the MSC had a policy which aimed to 'encourage both boys and girls to consider opportunities in areas traditionally entered by one sex or the other the reality was far different. The MSC itself showed a tendency to blame the entrants themselves for the situation. A review of the special programmes thought that the attitudes of the young school leavers led to this situation. Undoubtedly such arguments have a kernel of truth. Many young women do not want to enter non-traditional jobs and are only too happy to enter the service sector rather than industry. They prefer to do office or shop work rather than deal with machinery or undertake manual work in building, painting, decorating or mechanics. Such responses are clearly the product of our educational system and of general social attitudes. Yet the attitudes of young school leavers are far from being the only explanation of what happened in the MSC YOP scheme. Indeed, MSC-funded research also pointed to ways in which MSC staff were also at fault, especially many of those in the closest contact with the entrants, as well as the staff of sponsors of the programme. Many of these staff knew little of the MSC's stated policy of opening up opportunities for women or actively supported it. Brelsford *et al* (Brelsford etal, 1982) found that women were not encouraged to consider non-traditional areas but instead were usually steered towards sex-stereotyped occupations. This reflected the general social attitudes of the staff but also other elements. Trainers were reluctant to suggest non-traditional work in some cases because they were trying to win the confidence of the entrants who they perceived as closely influenced by general attitudes. On other occasions entrants who were interested in non-traditional work lacked the confidence to say so and were afraid of being made fun of. A process of mutual stereotyping was operating. Other staff were unwilling to have girls enter non-traditional areas because they considered them unsuitable for the work. Lifting heavy weights in building work, for instance, was thought to be beyond a female's capabilities, whilst if girls were taken on many thought that employers would never accept them and that therefore they were denying an opportunity to a boy who might have a chance of future employment

In such situations many obstacles were placed in frot of girls
who did want to enter non-traditional areas:

> For example, one girl wanted to join the local authority main-
> tenance department, which was all-male. They objected at
> first on the grounds that the work was too heavy. Two girls
> who attended motor bike maintenance were only involved by
> the tutor when he suggested that they re-upholster the seat.
> (Brelsford, 1983)

It seems therefore that the YOP scheme not only failed to
meet the objectives of the MSC itself in relation to the development of further opportunities for women in employment but
that the organisation of, structures and staff in the scheme
were involved in limiting some of the opportunities that were
available. These constraints then reinforced the problems
already created by the generally gender-stereotypical
approach of many of the employers who were part of the
work-experience programme.

Obviously, despite this overall patterning some women did
get the opportunity to enter non-traditional areas. The gender-
stereotyping was typical of the scheme in general but did not
apply to every single entrant. Yet even when women did get
the opportunity to enter such areas there were problems.
Sexual harassment can always be a problem for women and
the younger you are the more difficult it can be to handle it
without losing confidence. One description of training courses
gives a feeling of the problems non-traditional entrants face:

> However much you think this that or the other person has
> accepted you can do all these things and we actually form
> some sort of friendship on that basis, it always comes out.
> Actually they can't tolerate equality. They can't accept I'm not
> a sex object – men of any age. . . .

> I find the whole canteen situation horrific. I can't walk any-
> where, I can't look anywhere, I can't do anything but I'm under
> observation.

> The way they (male trainees) treat the women in the canteen
> really embarrasses me. They don't seem to see them existing as
> people. (Lewisham, 1982)

Yet despite such problems the effort occasionally seems worthwhile, particularly when its the very 'feminised' characteristics attached to women that help them make it into a 'male' area:

> A lot of the time, the boys have to ask me, you know, 'What do I do now' and that sort of thing. Sometimes certain things like lacing. I look at mine and it's all neat, and I look at theirs and I think, well, it does make you feel better doesn't it (YOPS wiring trainee). (Lewisham, 1982)

When the YOP programme was finally brought to an end it was not, however, the failure of the scheme to deal with the problems of female entrants that lay behind its replacement. Instead it was more general issues. Trade unionists and the voluntary sector were increasingly critical of a scheme which more and more took on the appearance of being about employers' interests, about job substitution and cheap labour, rather than about training, skills and the individual. Young people themselves were becoming increasingly cynical and there were signs that they were no longer so interested in participating in the programme (Fairley, 1982). This widespread criticism was also fuelled by the increasing recession and the corresponding fall in the success rate of the programme in terms of getting young people into jobs. There had often been high success rates in the early days when the recession had not made its full impact and when the inadequacies of individuals could more clearly be blamed for the failure to get employment. The change in this situation and the fall from around an 80 per cent success rate to one that was as low as 20 per cent in some areas made the weaknesses of the scheme even more apparent. Criticism could no longer be deflected by eventual job placement.

In 1981, against this background of criticism and protest, the MSC issued a consultative document on training reform, the New Training Initiative (NTI) and a White Paper on the NTI came from the government in December that year. This White Paper allowed for a Youth Task Group to be set up to work out details of a new youth scheme that would replace YOP, expanding the programme and turning it into 'real' or 'quality' training. Controversy was raised over some of the government's proposals, including suggestions that young people should be compelled to take part in the scheme and that the cash allowances to be paid to those on the scheme should be lower than the already low levels paid to those participating in YOP. These elements were removed by the Task Group and the scheme that resulted was the Youth Training Scheme which came into operation in the autumn of 1983. However, the YTS itself was, and remains, only one element within the NTI, which was also concerned with the development of skill training and apprenticeships as well as opening up opportunities for adults in or out of work in order to update their knowledge and skills. All of this also involved a move towards more vocationally oriented education in schools, a task that the MSC has subsequently come to have a hand in.

Perhaps one of the most important elements in the new scheme was its permanence. The original youth unemployment programmes had been set up by the Special Programmes division of the MSC and reflected the point of view that the task was something 'special', out of the usual run of things, dealing with problems that most young people would not face, providing the skills and experience that only a few unfortunates had failed to acquire. The report on the Youth Task Group, on the other hand, stressed that the emphasis was not now on unemployment per se but concerned all young people: 'This report is about providing a permanent bridge between school and work. It is not about youth unemployment' (Youth Task Group, 1982). The NTI therefore wanted to move towards a situation where all young people under the age of 18 would have the opportunity of continuing full-time education or of entering training or a period of planned work experience combining work-related training and education. With the element of compulsion removed this meant that new schemes would also have to appear significantly different and a more attractive proposition than the YOP schemes had turned out to be.

The YTS could not totally meet the criteria of offering all those under 18 a place on the programme at first, but undertook that all minimum-age school leavers remaining unemployed would be offered a place and that some 26-year-olds in jobs would also get opportunities through the scheme. It was also hoped that opportunities would be opened up for some of those who left school at 17 and became unemployed, and that disabled 18-year-olds would have access to the scheme as well. Around 460,000 places were created on the YTS for 1983/4, 300,000 of these on Mode A schemes and 160,00 on Mode B schemes. The Mode A schemes are employer-based schemes. The schemes are organised and supervised by managing agents who can be private employers, a group of employers or local authorities. The Mode B schemes fall into two groups, both of which are for the unemployed. Mode B1 schemes take place in training workshops, community projects and in the 44 Information and Technology Centres (ITEC). Mode B2 schemes are implemented from Further Education colleges and link work experience with off-the-job training and education. Many smaller employers can be drawn into the YTS through this scheme. The predominance of the Mode A schemes reflect the Government's commitment to seeing training as something that, above all, involves employers and employers' needs. As David Young, the then chairman of the MSC, said in 1982:

> Training is about work-related skills and is intimately concerned with employment. It is for this reason that training in this country must be employer-dominated and ultimately employer – directed.   (Young, 1982)

The result of this perspective on training has been that even within one year of the scheme coming into operation there have been cut-backs on Mode B places and attempts to expand Mode A employer – based programmes. This pattern of development has already led to some complaints that a two-tier system is emerging, with Mode A schemes regarded as high status and Mode B schemes as lower status. Such distinctions can then become linked to other social inequalities and at least one local study has suggested it is significant that in the schemes under examination the Mode A scheme's population was white and middle class and the Mode B scheme's participants predominately black and more working class (Farish, 1984).

The establishment of the YTS in which the unions – who

had been so critical of YOPS – participated, has not passed without critical attention. The labour movement itself is divided, with the leadership mainly committed to cautious support and expressing the intention of monitoring the scheme to prevent the kinds of abuses that took place on YOP. Union representatives sit on the Area Manpower Boards that have been established to vet applications for the scheme. However, some of the criticisms that are voiced go further than a concern with possible abuses of the scheme and relate the whole development of training schemes for young people to the political and economic concerns of the Conservative administration, and to the general economic system of which Britain is part. The Greater London Training Board, for instance, has argued that:

> The Government is undertaking a step-by-step plan of action, described in veiled terms in the NTI and is transforming the labour market by stealth on behalf of the employer's interests.
>
> (GLTB, 1984)

Training is being devalued and at the same time control of policy being centralised, removing all control except that of the Government and exployers:

> trade unions, local education authorities, training centres, Industrial Training boards, skill centres, standard setting bodies are all being systematically undermined.
>
> (GLTB, 1984, p. 28)

Meanwhile, despite the obvious fact that the labour market cannot produce the number of jobs required, an emphasis is still being placed on the inadequacies of the individual, all of whom will now be offered training when they leave school and who will internalise the reasons for their failure as they have had an opportunity for 'training' but still not made good (GLTB, 1984). The White Paper on the NTI still claimed a mismatch between the numbers of skilled workers required by a modern competitive economy and what was actually being produced. Despite a massive rise in unemployment there was still a promise of a bright future which required a 'better educated, better trained and more adaptable workforce to

take advantage of the opportunities presented by new technology, (A New Training Initiative, 1981). A leap is made
from this bright future to the realities of existing schemes
where the educational content, the experience and particularly
the notion of adaptability have been treated far more cyni-
cally. The training that the MSC offers is argued to be 'a
training in social skills, in a willingness to be adaptable and to
accept taking a variety of intermittent jobs' (Moos, 1983), part
of an onslaught on patterns of existing skill training like
apprenticeship where unions have a strong element of control,
as well as being a slick exercise in number manipulation,
removing school leavers from the dole queue and feeding them
back to employers as low-paid trainees (Finn, 1983). From this
perspective the NTI and the establishment of the YTS have to
be set firmly in the context of the policies of the existing Conservative administration, with whom not even the MSC has
seen eye to eye on occasion. The debate no longer seems one
about an objective 'good' training policy but is concerned with
the belief in the free market, in voluntarism in relation to
training, about employers' 'needs' and about moving obstruc-
tions from the operations of these forces, including such
'obstacles' as unions and Industrial Training Boards.

How then do equal opportunities fit into the development of
the YTS and which perspective on the YTS do developments
in this area reinforce – the belief in skills for the future, or the
view that sees a scheme aimed at isolating the labour movement and where 'young people will be trained passively to
accept poverty and unemployment' (Fairley, 1982)? To some
observers there seemed ground for hoping that the establishment of the YTS would prove of importance to women. The
Youth Task Group Report stated that:

> They will expect the scheme to treat young people taking part
> in the scheme both fairly and equitably. It will of course, need
> to comply with existing legislation forbidding discrimination
> but, more than this, should provide positive opportunities for
> disadvantaged groups.   (Youth Task Group, 1982).

For some this suggested that if the YTS was used positively it
could help bring about changes in sex stereotyped employment
patterns and open up new opportunities to women. The EOC,

however, and feminist groups involved in training had been more reticent in their reaction to the NTI, feeling that equal opportunities had not been properly grasped as an issue, whilst one of the researchers into the problems of YOPs for female entrants wrote in 1983:

> Some programme assessors have already suggested that in the rush to launch YTS equal opportunities will be relegated to a very low place on the agenda. Lets hope this pessimistic picture is not confirmed by events.   (Brelsford, 1983)

Unfortunately this pessimism appears to be well-justified by subsequent events.

Girls have not entered the YTS in equal numbers with boys. At the end of 1983 the breakdown was 119, 681 boys in Mode A schemes compared to 94,295 girls; in the Mode B schemes there were 58,140 boys to 32, 183 girls (WNC, 1984). Once within the scheme it appears that the familiar problem of gender stereotyping appeared almost immediately. In Mode A schemes employers are meant to be offering the training. All the YTS opportunities are for a year and involve a three-month off-the-job training and education element which need not be taken in a block but can be taken in the form of day release. Participants in YTS are taken on by employers as 'trainees' not employees, they receive a state allowance not wages, and do not have full protection under the employment laws. Employers can also offer YTS-funded training to 16-year-olds that they have already employed but only in a set proportion of permanent employees to temporary YTS trainees. As the figures above show the majority of YTS places are in these Mode A schemes, and the fact that they are determined and run by the employer even though the educational element may be farmed out to other establishments means that straight away the existing gender-stereotypical occupational patterning of employment in Britain will have an effect. Girls and boys are being introduced into work situations which are strongly stereotyped. The fact that the schemes are in operation for a year makes it difficult to offer non-traditional opportunities to either sex, for few are likely to have the confidence or commitment to undertake non-traditional experience unless special provision is made, including, for instance, the possibility of sampling a non-traditional role for a few weeks of the scheme rather than making a once-and-for-all decision for the year. However, this would mean an effort by the employers, whether public or private, and it is the employers who have been pinpointed as being part of their problem by their deep-rooted attitudes towards the role of women in employment. It seems unlikely that in the swift transition from YOP to YTS any thorough attempt was made to transform these attitudes which some MSC staff were very often in tune with. Very few of the opportunities, therefore, would avoid the existing pattern of segregation. Very seldom are there schemes which would escape from traditional mental categories and therefore attract both boys and girls. The result has been a clear pattern of gender segregation within the scheme. In Devon and Cornwall, for instance, female entrants made up 95 per cent of those in the personal service and sale sector, 73 per cent in the administrative and clerical sector but 0.6 per cent in the installation, maintenance and repair group (WNC, 1984). It seems clear that despite commitments by the MSC at the start of YTS to equal opportunities for girls the result has been not quite equal access in terms of numbers and a very clear continuance of gender stereotyping.

Yet whilst Mode A schemes are under the direction of employers or their managing agents the Mode B schemes generally have the MSC itself as the managing agent and therefore the MSC should be able to make more impact on opportunities for women in this sector of the YTS. Yet if we look at Mode B schemes the closer they come to areas that could roughly regarded as technical or 'masculinised', the fewer women there are. Women had only 31 per cent of the places in training workshops under Mode B and women made up only 27 per cent of those in ITECs. Of course, the existence of this pattern in the first year of the scheme's operation does not necessarily mean that the problem is permanent or unsolvable. The MSC has promised to monitor the number of girls entering the scheme and the patterning that results. It is looking into pilot schemes for examples of good practice and making available special training material both for its own and for sponsors' staff which would increase awareness of equal opportunities issues and the need for special activities in this area. The Commission talks of ensuring that general publicity is favourable to and attractive to girls as well as boys and that entrance criteria should be structured so as to relate to general motivation and ability rather than the possession of particular qualifications which could lead to indirect discrimination against girls. On the other hand the MSC have refused to set quotas for girls in YTS on the basis of the argument that the aim should not to be to achieve success in numerical terms but rather to ensure that girls who want to enter non-traditional areas are not stopped from doing so just because they are female (WNC, 1984, Appendix C).

Attempts to enlarge the scope for women's training so far have to be considered against this background. Mode B schemes, for example, would seem to have an important part to play in opening up opportunities for women precisely because as the managing agent the MSC would be in a position to put some of its paper commitments into practice. Yet the numbers of women in these schemes are a smaller percentage of the total than on Mode A schemes and it is also the Mode B schemes that are being closed down. The commitment by the government to employer-led training with the goal of putting 'British business back on its feet' has led to pressure to increase the employer-related places on Mode A and to close down schemes under Mode B. Community schemes, in particular, have come under heavy pressure. Community projects were cut back by nearly 30 per cent within four months of the start of YTS (Youthaid, 1984). Yet in many cases these were long-established schemes that had come into the YTS, which were popular with young people and which even had waiting lists (Youthaid, 1984 b). Closure of Mode B schemes therefore limits the possibilities of more rapidly developing places that could benefit women. The ITECS (Information Technology Centres) are one part of Mode B that have not suffered from cuts, however. The existing Conservative Government's belief in new technology appears to protect them, and the centres, jointly funded by the MSC and the Department of Trade and Industry, are planned to expand in number. Yet even in such a high-profile area and one which seems most in tune with some of the dreams and plans of the New Training Initiative there appear to be problems. The Greater London Training Board has argued that:

> ITECs are often not funded or housed properly, the standard of training is not consistent and there needs to be careful scrutiny to ensure that girls are not ghettoised in wordprocessing options with little chance of a job in the future and boys concentrated in electronics and computing operations.
>
> (GLTB, 1984)

The development of such a pattern would not be surprising in light of the general tendency to segregate areas of work in new technology.

The fact that attention is being switched to Mode A schemes is, to many observers, likely to result in a replication of the inadequacies and problems that plagued the Youth Opportunities Programme, and, therefore, the continuance of the same problems in relation to the way in which women are treated in the scheme:

> Many observers of the YTS are worried that under the Managing Agency system the scheme will be geared too much towards the interests of the sponsor rather than the trainee. Managing agents who themselves act as sponsors, or whose interest in the scheme is simply as a profit-making business operation, may not impose the strict standards of training quality, course structure, trainee rights, equal opportunities and scheme safety that were promised by the Task Group Report on which the YTS is supposedly based.
>
> The MSC has done little to alleviate these fears. There has been no assurance that every workplace will even be visited. Senior officials continue to express their confidence that managing agents will maintain high standards, and point to the contracts that they have signed with the MSC. Yet on YOP, abuses such as the substitution of trainees for adult workers and failure to provide adequate safety facilities, directly contravened agreements made between sponsors and the MSC and in some cases broke the law. Better standards are unlikely to be achieved on YTS without a more direct MSC presence on individual schemes.
>
> (Youthaid, 1984)

The fact that there are few women amongst MSC staff and the Managing Agents or on the Area Management Boards is seen as yet another problem with the YTS in relation to women's opportunities. Of course, being a women does not automatically make a person sympathetic to the problems facing female entrants to YTS. Many women can be, and are, socially conservative and are happy to see women succeed in areas that are seen as the 'right sphere' for women. On the other hand it is possible that women who have had to fight their way into non-traditional areas already, who have experienced some of the problems, who have made it into management or into the trade union hierarchy and know the forms of discrimination and institutionalised discrimination that they themselves have had to make a way through, would be more sensitive to the needs of women and more willing to bring the problems of equal opportunities to the forefront. The Women's National Commission think this is particularly important in relation to the area management boards who have the task of assessing the nature and quality of the opportunities that are needed, mobilising local support, supervising the managing agents and agreeing budgets and policies within their areas. Yet women are very under-represented in these boards. The MSC only appointed 7 women as chairpersons of the boards out of 54 and both the TUC and the CBI, who can nominate 5 members each to the boards, have failed to even achieve one woman on each board (WNC, 1984).

Why is there this gap between the formal commitments of the MSC to opening up opening up opportunities for girls in the YTS and what seems to be happening in the schemes on the ground? Why, despite repeated commitments by the Commission, is gender stereotyping still occurring? Part of the answer undoubtedly lies in the wider social context, in the attitudes employers, trainers and trainees bring to the scheme. But on the other hand attitudes are not necessarily permanent, nor is it necessary to sit back and wait for the whole of society to undergo a slow metamorphosis in the way women are regarded and treated in society – a change which many institutional and organisational structures are working against.

One part of the answer must lie in the fact that the employment and unemployment of women is not yet considered to be a politically important issue. This is not to say that women's unemployment is unimportant, nor that the economy as it is currently structured does not benefit from existing stereotyped patterns. Clearly women's employment is important. The largest expansion in employment since the last World War has been in employment for women, especially in part-time work. Employers benefit from this situation in many ways, the fact that women are still paid lower rates than men, despite the Equal Pay Act, being but one of these. In some industries the fact that women are part-time places them outside many of the benefit contributions that employers would have to make for them if they were full-time, thus saving the employer further money. The fact that many women are available for shift work, fitting it round their family commitments is also beneficial to some industries and occupations, whilst for some employers women can be used as a disposable labour force which can be easily shed in times of economic trouble. In other industries older women act as a hard core of permanent, committed workers (Breughel, 1979; Coyle, 1984; Perkins, 1983; West, 1982). Despite this centrality of women to the current labour market in Britain, women remain invisible in other respects. Many of them disappear off the unemployment register back into the home. Others are the subject of cynical manouevrings to bring this about. They are not a subject for political concern, whatever the party, and when a return to full employment is envisaged, this return is very much conceptualised in terms of male employment (Phillips, 1984). It means that if political plans are made for the restructuring and resurgence of the economy then the kind of job opportunities that are sought are conceptualised in male terms. It is precisely such assumptions that lie behind the continuing dominance of a belief in the need for a family wage, the wage that will allow a man to keep a dependent wife, despite the fact that empirically this pattern applies to only a tiny percentage of the population. Women are just not seen as part of the political problem and, of course, these attitudes are reinforced not only by the general social orientation towards the role of women but by the ideas about their relation to technology and skill that were discussed in Chapter 1. Women, even if they are to enter the labour force and if this fact is acknowledged, are not generally thought of as requiring training.

This produces a slight contradiction around the area of the YTS for the emphasis upon youth in general suggests that women are included in the scheme and that they too require the sort of 'quality training' that the YTs is supposed to be providing. But it is not unusual for contradictory concepts to be operating in society and the parallel existence of both notions suggests both why women are included in the programme but also why there is no firm commitment in practice to ensuring that their needs are met.

A more material reason that should also be considered is the question of how such a commitment could be met in practice, the resources it would involve and the role that the state in the form of the MSC would have to play. All the evidence so far has shown that to genuinely open up opportunities to women would require large-scale intervention by the MSC. It would cost money in terms of training the trainees and sponsors, but perhaps more importantly, it would also involve placing constraints upon the employers in the Mode A schemes who are failing to attune their programmes to MSC equal opportunities criteria. The constraints placed upon employers could take many forms. There could, for example, be the refusal of funds unless equal opportunity criteria were met. This, though, could lead to a rapid withdrawal of some employers from the scheme if they saw no reason to alter their existing policies. Whatever the form of pressure or persuasion that was tried the most important fact about it would be that it goes against the current Conservative administration's commitment to employer-led training, to voluntarism and to the rolling back of the state – the state being regarded as already too deeply involved in the structure of people's lives and particularly too deeply involved in economic structures to the detriment of a free market. Precisely such attitudes lie behind the privatisation of many of the nationalised industries. From this perspective intervention into the employers' area of concern would be unthinkable.

CHAPTER 5

Further Education

For many people training takes place when they leave school, and this has certainly been the major growth area for the MSC. The MSC's schemes, originally invoked to assist in the transition from school to work for small numbers of people who lacked qualifications that would help them get work, has now expanded so much that it is hoped – even if this has yet to occur in practice – to provide all school leavers with the opportunity to enter a training programme on leaving school (apart, that is, from those going into higher education). For the moment, only some of our school leavers get access to training through the MSC when leaving school. Others go into further education which is itself becoming more intertwined with the MSC, as the MSC has come to be a major source of finance for this sector of the education system. However, the training provided this way is not the only form of training that is available and in other cases training can be provided once people have actually gained employment rather than before they start. In such circumstances the further education sector can also be involved, for day – release students find their courses provided for them in such FE colleges. In other occupations the training can be provided within firms themselves either in a formally established course, by 'sitting next to Nellie', or through a wide variety of experiences within work which are themselves defined as being part of the training needed for promotion.

In many cases such training and the elements of experience

which are seen as counting as part of future work preparation are linked to internal labour markets. Internal labour markets are often within a firm, although it is argued that they can also be within an occupation (Ford, 1984). They are characterised by a hierarchy of jobs through which people are promoted and entry into this hierarchy is only at the bottom, at the point when you actually start employment with the firm or institution. Movement up the hierarchy is then equated with the acquisition of knowledge and skill. A lot of debate has gone on around the notion of internal labour markets and has particularly centred around the question of whether internal labour markets are favoured by management because they help ensure a stable labour force and weaken the working class, whether they can also offer disadvantages to employers, and whether the system offers both employers and workers mutual advantages. Whatever the outcome of this debate, statistical evidence does suggest that internal labour markets are becoming increasingly important. (In 1977 31 per cent of employers used them for the recruitment of manual workers, compared to 13 per cent in 1973; for non-manual workers the figures were 52 per cent in 1977 compared to 21 per cent in 1973 (Ford etal, 1984)). Within particular companies internal labour markets can run right through firms – you come in as a typist or an office junior and work your way up to the top of the firm – or they can be confined to specific areas of the firm – you enter as a typist and could possibly work your way up to supervisor of the typing pool but you couldn't then move on to managing the firm. Internal labour markets are also to be found in many different occupations, from industrial manufacturing processes to banking.

The development and forms of differentiation of these internal labour markets are important for women workers because it is in the occupations which have them, either right the length of the firm or just in sub-sections of them, that opportunities for women seem to exist.

However, a closer examination shows that across a wide variety of occupations employers treat women in a different way from men, limiting their access to forms of training and therefore to forms of promotion within these internal labour markets. The differentiation that employers or superiors display towards men and women applies even where sex discrimination is formally seen as a problem and formal declarations of intent are made to try and remove it. Attitudes, in particular, are not so easily changed or eradicated and continue to be one of the main problems in developing opportunities for women. Such attitudes lead not only to a situation where women are denied access to training and therefore to promotion but also to the imposition of forms of qualification, patterns of experience, and kinds of acknowledged expertise that are applicable only to men and not to women. These therefore exclude women from the career structure of occupations. This pattern of experience obviously takes specific forms in different occupations in different places, individual justifications and experiences are all subtly diverse. Yet whether we consider manual or non-manual work, industry, service or clerical occupations, there do appear to be shared features which can be identified and which have not only to be identified but also to be overcome if women are to get the forms of training which are shaped to their requirements and which are to give them the fullest opportunities.

There are two main problems facing women in any form of internal labour market: the first is that of getting access to the training in the first place; the second lies in the form and content of the training that is provided. The first problem, getting access to training, has to be seen as part of the training process itself. Getting women into programmes whether they are in colleges, in skill centres or in firms, has to be regarded as an integral part of the training process, an important part of its structure. It is no use laying on schemes that would suit women down to the ground if women either don't hear about them, haven't the confidence to enter them or otherwise find their way blocked. This is a recurring problem with all the forms of training considered in this book, but it shows up especially clearly in some of the internal labour markets, especially in areas such as banking where formally discrimination has been removed.

If we take banking as an example it is clear that despite the existence of a Sex Discrimination Act in Britain there are policies still current inside the banking system which act to help reproduce the general social picture of ghettoisation and clustering at low levels for women. Seventy-five percent of the women in banks are clerical employees, 37 per cent are supervisors and administrators, 5 per cent have made it to lower and middle management, but none have managed to get into higher management. That this situation need not be so can be indicated by reference to France where comparable figures are 57 per cent, 43 per cent, 36 per cent and 8 per cent (Povall, 1984, p. 35). That is, in France, 8 per cent of the female employees there have made it into the higher levels of management. This is a far from perfect situation for women but it does serve to indicate that such career prospects need not be impossible, as they seem to be in Britain. The size of the problem appears even more clearly when we realise that since the start of the 1970s women have, in fact, constituted around 55 per cent of all bank employees (Egan, 1982, p. 21)

One important feature of banking, as of many other internal labour markets, is that there is usually one point of entry and that it is usually only young people who are recruited. Very few older women are taken into employment by the banks. For instance in 1979 only 3.3 per cent of the female entrants into Williams and Glyns banks were over 40 per cent (Egan, 1982, p. 27). If older women do come in they will come in at the lower grades and will remain there: their age will prevent them from being considered for entry onto a career ladder. Even the small number of women that do come into bank work or return to it later in life are not catered for in promotional terms. Yet the rules that often bar them are written as general rules and not aimed obviously at women alone. For instance National Westminster in 1979 would not allow any of its employees over 30 study leave time for IOB (Institute of Banking) Examinations at part 2, stage 2 (Egan, 1982, p. 26). This meant that late entrants or women returning to work after a break for a family who had originally not looked for a career but now thought in terms of promotion would find their way blocked. If age barriers are one problem that women face in getting access to careers, we still have to explain why the many women who enter banking in their youth do not get on.

Once women are inside the banks promotion is related to training and the combination of internal training schemes, work experience and the Institute of Bankers professional qualifications gained through study and examinations. Access to all the elements of this combination is through management judgement and discretion and here the problem of attitudes becomes important. Many managers appear to believe that equal opportunity exists and that women can't or won't take the opportunities open to them (Povall, 1984, p. 36). Yet many of their female employees are well aware that their seniors are not so open in practise:

> Getting married this year didn't help my promotion prospects
>
> If you're a woman and married . . . they think that women get pregnant so they're not so keen on promoting, my section clerk actually said that.
>
> When I joined the bank I asked to do them (i.e. the banking examinations) and they said I wouldn't need them.
>
> (Crompton and Jones, 1984, pp. 159–60)

First job placements are also important. There is evidence that men are never placed in the secretarial jobs but that only a very few women are placed in the jobs within banks that are themselves seen as 'training' jobs with future prospects.

The limitation – one which is to be found in many organisations – on the age at which you can start training has further repercussions for women. Although they are being frozen out of many opportunities by the attitudes of their superiors many women are also likely to be entering work, as we know, with marriage and childrearing as their goal rather than an employment career. Some women obviously want both from the start and find their way blocked, but others may only realise that they would like a career later and then find that they're too old, even while still in their twenties:

> About a year ago they said I couldn't get promotion 'cos I didn't have the bank's exams and I was too old for day release. They offered a correspondence course – but that's no use to me.

Management attitudes can not only mean that women are not encouraged to take up the opportunities supposedly lying there open to them, it can also mean that the qualifications required for career advancement and promotion are applied more rigorously to women than to men (Wilkins, 1983, p. 29). It can also mean that the things that management look for in their workers and which they see as appropriate in those that are to have access to training and promotion are attributes that are very much constructed in male terms. Elements like 'fitting into a company' can often mean things like sport, and the sports concerned are male sports (Crompton and Jones, 1984, p. 244). As the general discussion of the notion of 'skill' in Chapter I has indicated, very often the characteristics and qualities that women display in their work go unnoticed and unrewarded. When recruitment and access to training pro- grammes rely on subjective judgements by superiors, by selec- tion and invitation, rather than by objective criteria, the situation will continue to work against women and lower their chances of access to training. If no women or very few women enter, then the whole thing becomes a self-fulfilling prophecy and women are seen as 'uninterested' in the opportunities supposedly open to them. Of course, the intro- duction of 'objective' criteria does not necessarily mean that the position for women will automatically change and the situation become rosy. We have already seen that supposedly 'objective' calculations in job evaluation schemes tend to always work to the detriment of women. Whilst if school gained qualifications are used as the criteria there still remains the problem of the many disadvantages that women find themselves in within the educational system. However, a move towards the establishment of objective criteria for access plus the development of work to try and effect changes in management attitudes and assumptions could open up many more training opportunities for women. Such changes are not impossible and could include elements tried elsewhere in Europe, such as: requests to management for statistics on attendance at training courses by women; discussion of the differences between branches or regions; bank targets for a percentage of women to be promoted; courses and equal opportunity discussions for those in positions to control everyday access to forms of training, etc.

There is also the problem to be faced of the imposition of other qualifications for promotion which act against the interests of women. If women see that there are criteria which they cannot or are unwilling to fill and which will act as a career blockage, then it is unlikely that they will be interested in undertaking actual training courses or sitting for examinations which will never lead them anywhere. The demand for mobility is one example of this kind of criteria. Many companies with career structures supposedly open to women such as banks or building societies also operate a branch network with branches and offices all over the country. The experience necessary for promotion, the diversity of tasks that have to be undertaken, is often assumed to be only possible thorough geographical mobility, by actually moving from branch to branch, whilst promotion itself involves moves from office to office. Yet this does not always have to be the case. Some building societies are beginning to recognise this and arrange for moves within a town or within a small radius for instance. In a study of a Belgian bank it was found that a commitment to geographical mobility was only required of a small number of managers and potential managers and therefore more women were able to reach positions of some responsibility. Small facts like these are of importance for training, for it has to be recognised that women still assume the greater domestic responsibilities and find that family ties and partners' jobs make geographical mobility difficult, if not impossible. From this perspective then, we begin to see that training cannot be considered in isolation from the social factors that structure women's perception of the use it will be to them. If mobility remains a criterian then examination results and training courses will all be useless. Any attempt to transform women's opportunities in training therefore has also to come to terms with this wider environment and find ways of identifying and removing these other obstacles.

However, these kinds of problems are associated with internal labour markets within a firm where there is at least a formal commitment to mobility, the offering of a career structure which goes through to the upper levels of management. But there are also internal labour markets, specifically those relating to just one occupational sector of a firm, that also create problems for women in relation to training.

As the general national statistical picture of women's employment indicates, most women are likely to find themselves at the bottom of any employment hierarchy and occupying the lower grades of jobs, few of which are regarded as comparable with male work. When there are opportunities for promotion and training it will be within these low level women's jobs and there will seldom be any opportunities to move into higher job categories or to transfer skills. In many cases, especially in industrial sectors, the training that is offered will be related to supervision rather than the technical content of the job. Initial training on entry is often minimal in many occupations and can be more a case of practice than any acquisition of technical skill. When further training is offered in the form of short courses it is usually related to promotion, and promotion in such confined internal female-dominated labour markets usually means a move into some form of supervisory capacity. Training then will be 'designed to improve their capacity to control and instruct other women; not to increase their technical knowledge' (Wilkins, 1983, p. 27).

Such a situation, of course, only applies where there is space in the hierarchy for female supervisors. In many cases supervisory posts are reserved for male workers. If women already have the ability to do their existing job and have nowhere else to go within the firm there is no stimulus for them to be interested in training. Even when they are interested and ambitious the lack of future opportunities makes women give up:

> I wouldn't mind going further in this job . . . but on the test side, all the supervisors are male (Wilkins, 1983, p. 28)

– was the rueful comment of one female electrical tester in an engineering firm.

In industrial firms, too, the forms of discrimination that operate to the disadvantage of women in white-collar jobs are also visible. Age limits for training and day release are to be found. Similarly there is no recognition of the problems of those returning to work, not all of whom are uninterested in the opportunities for further advancement and responsibility in employment. Where the opportunities for training are available the same problems of subjective criteria and judgement being involved in opportunities for access to training also apply. Many managers, for instance, operate as gatekeepers, choosing those who will have the chance to go on. A policy which, though it might give opportunities for a favoured few, can also lead to resentment and frustration for those not included. The establishment of objective criteria for choosing candidates for training could help to remove this problem. When women are picked rather than encouraged to choose, when it is relationships with one person further up the hierarchy that determine opportunity rather than encouragement to all, then it is not surprising that many women do not even consider the possibilities for further training. They are not in a context which is likely to promote such considerations. This in itself points to the importance of both establishing criteria for access to training and of widely publicising them, and encouraging consideration of the opportunities within the whole relevant population.

Another problem facing those who wish to expand women's training opportunities is less amenable to resolution by any immediate actions or good training practice. When Paul Willis did a study of boys at school, looking at the way in which working-class youth had only limited social mobility and therefore tended to end up in working-class jobs, he distinguished between the 'ear' oles' and the 'lads'. The former were those who conformed within the school, the latter group were those who tended to be disruptive in the classroom from the point of view of the school authorities. Willis regarded this second group as actually the ones being realistic. They'd recognised that the school ethos and the emphasis on examinations were, in fact, irrelevant to the way in which they were going to spend their future and that the kind of work environment that they were likely to enter in fact valued the kind of assertive, jokey masculinity that appeared disruptive within a school setting (Willis, 1977). In the same way it can be

recognised that women are, on many occasions, rejecting
training opportunities that appear open to them because they
can see that acquiring qualifications and skills through training
wouldn't get them anywhere. In some cases this will be
because of gender segregation in the workplace. Training
would make them qualified for work that men already occupy
within a firm and it would require a commitment by the management of the firm to positively encourage moves into these
areas to open up opportunities rather than any effort by individual female workers to acquire the necessary qualifications.
On other occasions the problem may lie in the labour process
itself, in the actual work, its content and organisation.
Women may get trained and then find that they have no
opportunity to put any of the skills and competences they
have acquired into operation:

> They paid for day release and everything . . . but as I got more
> and more skilled, the job got less and less. (Wilkins, 1983,
> p. 28)

Where such situations exist there is no incentive for women to
apply for training unless they can hope to get employment in
another firm where these skills would be used. The end result
is likely to be either a situation where women are unwilling to
train, or one where they have to leave when trained and where
the employers are therefore likely to be unwilling to provide
the opportunities for day release or the finance, for both of
these are investments in workers, in labour power, that they
will lose when that worker moves on.

None of the problems outlined here in relation to training
opportunities for women are insurmountable, whether the
internal labour markets are within firms, or just in particular –
usually sex segregated – occupations within firms. The
exception is the one where the training does not match the
content of the job because this may require a far wider
reassessment and form of commitment, not to mention
expenditure, on the part of the employer than the other problems require. There are examples already available of good
practices which can be used to help remove some of the barriers
indicated above. In Pauline Wilkins's study of engineering

firms, for example, she found one company training scheme whose efforts went a long way towards resolving some of the problems women faced in relation to training opportunities. In the scheme she looked at:

> there was an open system of application and simple testing for entry, and all women were encouraged to apply;
>
> it was coordinated with promotion and work experiences;
>
> there were no age limits;
>
> there was an entry test rather than a demand for previous educational requirements, and as well as this there was an element of job related remedial education, especially in maths;
>
> there were two stages to encourage the less confident to apply.   (Wilkins, 1983)

When the scheme was examined some women were already in the second, higher stage and one women was already beginning to have ambitions to become not merely a technician (from being a semi-skilled worker) but a professional engineer. The sad footnote to this story is the fact that that scheme, so successful and dealing with so many of the problems facing women in relation to training, has already been curtailed as a result of the economic recession. Yet it is precisely in a recession, when female unemployment is rapidly increasing, that the already limited openings and opportunities for women are likely to be further curtailed and women need to have every avenue open to them if their situation is not to become worse than it already is.

In companies in areas such as banking, insurance or building societies, which are formally equal but on closer examination display many inadequacies in their treatment of women, changes in practice and an improvement in the situation of women are also possible. Just as they share some of the same problems with the industrial sectors so, too, are some of the solutions similar. Developments in both America and Europe have shown that changes are possible. One of the reasons the situation of women in French banks, while far from perfect, is better than that of women in British banks, for example, is precisely because some efforts have been made to deal with women's problems and to open up a career path in deed as well as in word.

Further Education

If, for some women, training opportunities are related to employment this can often involve attendence at institutes of further education. Day release, for instance has been a traditional part of apprenticeship. However, as well as day release there are many other forms of opportunity available through the further education sector, a sector which itself is becoming increasingly intertwined with the role and activities of the Manpower Services Commission.

The further education sector is itself a complex one, embracing a variety of institutions. Occasionally institutions like polytechnics are included in the the definition (see for example, Cantor, 1980) but here further education will be taken to be those institutions offering education below degree level. Although it is called the 'further education sector' this is traditionally the area of education that has been closest to the economy both through its links with apprenticeship and through the courses it provides, which are seen as having a strong technical content that is necessary for employment. The latter would include management courses, technical training, computing or secretarial activities, for example. However, precisely because of these links with the world of work this sector has traditionally been regarded as one of low status, a position which reflects the academic bias of the British education system and which runs contrary to present moves to encourage stronger links between schools and industry, between education and employment.

Today the education – training distinction is begining to disappear in this sector, mainly as a result of the activities of the Manpower Services Commission. Whilst further education in the past had been linked to employment, to actually providing opportunities outside the workplace for these in certain occupations, or else providing training that will lead to employment, the further education sector is now caught up in providing many courses for the MSC. For many commentators the move towards the provision of courses for the MSC is not a move towards preparing for employment but actually a means of dealing with unemployment. From this perspective:

> the mass extension of further education is seen to have less to do with equipping labour with specific technical skills to make it more employable, and more to do with establishing replacement criteria (vocational education, work experience, FE, and so forth,) for regulating the growing queue of young unemployed people awaiting entry into a contracting job market.
>
> (Gleeson, 1983, p. 37)

This perspective on the MSC is one that has been frequently voiced and has become more common as the recession deepens, job placements fall, and some of the inadequacies that were examined in the last chapter come to light.

This view of the MSC's activities is still a controversial one, but what does seem clear is that a tripartite system is developing in FE with the sector dealing with crafts and apprenticeship, operatives, typists, hairdressers, cooks etc.; a second sector which developed in the 1950's and 70's dealing with the tertiary, service and public areas and covering topics such as social work, management, get O and A levels, business etc., and which is seen as having an academic content; and a third sector which is where the MSC courses are to be found. The three sectors are very different, recruit different kinds of students, are preparing for different labour markets in essence, and have a very different status within the colleges – a status which spreads to the staff themselves. Those teaching the academic courses are regarded as somehow better than those involved in MSC courses, for instance. Furthermore such stratification operates very much like streaming in schools, making students very aware of differences between them.

Increasingly there seems to be a decline of the craft sector. In some cases the occupations themselves are being destroyed through the process of industrial restructuring and change. However, current attacks on the whole notion of apprenticeship by a Conservative-led government are also another factor in the decline in this area. Paradoxically, the decline of the craft sector can also mean less contacts with industry, paradoxical that is, in the context of the current emphasis on increasing contacts between education and industry. However, whilst this may be a political emphasis it can also be asked whether industry in fact cares. It has been suggested that employers recognise that many jobs are now routine ones that require little expertise and little or no further education and training, and that employers have shown remarkably little interest in vocational education and training beyond what is immediately profitable (Gleeson, 1983, p. 44). Indeed, it was industry's dismal record in the area of training that was responsible for state intervention in training policy in the 1960. The situation in general appears to have changed little in the intervening period.

Whilst the craft sector is declining in importance, that related to the MSC is increasing rapidly and finance has an important part to pay in this. The MSC policy of buying in courses from the colleges means that finance from the MSC has come to be an important part of many FE budgets. It is estimated that in general MSC money is now 8 per cent of the overall FE budget, but that in some areas of the country it represents as much as 70 per cent (Moos, 1983). Whilst money obviously talks and talks loudly in some areas the impact of the MSC also means that the FE sector is losing some of its formerly independent status. If a sector becomes dependent for money on an outside area then to some extent it also comes under the control of that area which determines the type of courses that are required.

However, if these are the general changes taking place in the FE sector what is the importance of this sector to women and what kinds of opportunities do they find there? The section on the role and development of the MSC has already shown that neither YOP nor the YTS has developed opportunities for women in any substantial way. It is not to be expected therefore that MSC courses bought in the colleges would be particularly different. However, it is clear the FE courses in general, not just those connected with the MSC, continue the process of gender-stereotyping of opportunities. In part this a continuation of a historical tradition. Whilst women have always been evident in FE, by 1975–6 constituting around 60 per cent of the student population in non-advanced FE (including evening institutes), there has also been a strong gender-stereotyping of their opportunities. In the 1890's the only kinds of vocational education open to women and girls were those connected with domestic science and whilst formal barriers to entry into other types of courses and experiences have disappeared the tradition of strong gender stereotyping remains (Blunden, 1983). Commentators on the FE sector agree that courses are still very much regarded by both staff and students as 'male' or 'female' courses. The figures clearly reflect such views. In 1979, for instance, men made up 99 per cent of those taking engineering subjects, and 99.6 per cent of those in the construction area. Women, on the other hand, were just as predominant in the commercial courses (Sammons, 1983, p. 120).

Part of this situation is due to the strong feelings of the students themselves. Studies have shown that gender is stronger than class in determining the courses taken (Sammons, 1983). Family and friends, often the main sources of knowledge and advice about employment, seldom challenge existing social choices. The end result is one where, even when FE teachers do try to challenge the stereotypes, they find the students resisting them:

> Well I started off the year by showing a film called 'Jobs for the Girls' . . . It's a film showing one young school leaver trying to get work as a car mechanic-woman, and the problems that she had in that. And I did start off the year with that film and a discussion about sex discrimination, about sexual socialisation, to give that sort of perspective in it (laugh) but it doesn't seem to have achieved very much. And I gear a lot of work into talking about that. Education, I've looked at again; socialisation in the education system, choice of subject and so on, but they are quite adamant that these are the subjects they want to do and this is a little bit irrelevant to them.
>
> (Avis, 1983, p. 208).

Obviously, not all students are so resistant: some girls are now studying science or engineering, for instance, but such choices remain the choice of the minority. That family is particularly important in helping to sustain this pattern is clear from studies of female engineering students. Again and again such studies have found that whether talking of technician level or degree level, having a role model at home, especially a father himself in engineering, is an important element in a woman deciding to enter such an occupation (Newton, 1981). However, the lack of such a role model or definite encouragement within the family is not a total determinant, and when courses are set up specifically to attract women into such areas, with an enrolment drive publicly trying to attract this group, many women can be attracted. However, such initiatives are, unfortunately, still few in number.

In the current context the colleges themselves seem to be the source of considerable problems in relation to women's opportunities. These problems are several and various. They range over a variety of issues from the lack of attempts to draw in women students into 'non traditional' areas, the failure to utilise women staff effectively, the structure of the courses themselves down to the lack of awareness by many members of staff of the importance of such issues (Stoney and Reid, 1981). In other words, far from helping to mitigate the effects of a difficult problem which has its roots in the existing education system and social values in general, the FE sector is playing a part in helping to ensure that the situation is reproduced and perpetuated.

The research study undertaken by Sheila Stoney and Margaret Reid for the Further Education Curriculum Review and Development Unit identified many of the ways in which the FE sector does this. College prospectuses still portray men and women pursuing 'traditional' courses (Blunden, 1983) as do many careers materials. Both admission interviews and subsequent classroom behaviour indicate that staff operate with perceptions, albeit unconscious ones, of appropriate courses, conduct and activities for men and for women. The evidence as to how teachers respond differently to males and to females in the classroom is perhaps still controversial, but there also seems to be evidence that what happens in the classroom is important because of the fact that men and women

Imp

appear to prefer to learn in different ways – women preferring more structured material and being more influenced by the method rather than the content of the teaching. A finding that, in relation to schools, has led on the discussions about whether single-sex classes might be more appropriate (see Smith, 1984). If women approach the teaching of courses differently there is also the suggestion that they perceive subjects differently and have a more humanistic approach to subjects. A study of Open University women students taking technology, for instance, found that the attraction was a desire to understand the environmental implications of technology and that in the course the environmental and energy-related aspects had been those found to be the most interesting (Swarbrick, 1982); a conclusion that seems in accord with studies of the attitudes of school-age girls and boys (Stoney and Reid, 1981, p. 15).

It became clear from the study by Stoney and Reid that changes in staff themselves will be an important element in introducing changes in FE which would widen opportunities for women. As many staff in FE are not trained as teachers, unlike those who work in schools, this task is all the more difficult because at least those who teach in schools can be alerted to the problems during their period of teacher training. In-service training courses may be one solution to this problem, but they appear an unlikely one in view of an overall move towards constraints on expenditure in the area of education. However, unless teachers are aware of the problems or an outside agency somehow intervenes along the lines of the GIST project (Girls into Science and Technology) in schools, supporting action research related to widening opportunities, the future appears to be fairly gloomy. Many of the ways that Stoney and Reid identify as possible means of aiding women depend on rethinking and reordering both the content and structure of courses. They give one example of how the very language of the curriculum could be changed to make its content more familiar and less alien whilst still dealing with the same knowledge and concepts:

'What is meant by the 'denaturation of protein by heat'? Explain the process using the effect of heat on egg protein to illustrate your answer.' Can be transformed, with equivalent meaning, into: 'Scrambled egg thickens with heat. Name this thickening process and explain how thickening takes place, using diagrams wherever possible.'

Another example they praised was where the teaching of physics had been deliberately structured to apply the theory to everyday examples with which the women students were familiar. However, these efforts and similar ones can only occur when staff are aware of the problem and willing to take action about it. Yet the same study found that in the majority of departments the staff talked of not making any distinctions, or of treating the male and female students equally, rather than being prepared to acknowledge that male and female students might have different needs in relation to study (Stoney and Reid, 1981, p. 35). Of course, not all the problems in breaking down gender stereotyping are the responsibility of staff. Other changes could also help. These are the more general ones that are problems in all other forms of training, especially when it involves opening opportunities to older women workers. Child-care facilities, putting courses within the boundaries of school hours, financial incentives, are all elements that have been continually identified as problems in relation to women; all of them however tend to involve finance and this remains a major problem in a recessionary period.

Many of these latter suggestions are ones that would help more women with existing domestic responsibilities, get access to further education and training. This could be important for there are tentative suggestions being made that attempts to open up 'non traditional' opportunities to women will not be very successful during the teen years, and that they should even be avoided for young girls at the moment. Tizard has argued, based on her own experience in trying to open up opportunities to women in engineering, that the situation between the sexes in the classroom is too much for many young girls to handle: at the stage when they would enter further education they still lack confidence in themselves and their own sexuality and therefore are more easily upset by the antagonism of the boys within the classroom. It is quite clear that such antagonism does exist, just as it does in many workplaces and throughout society at large, but she argues that slightly older women are more able to handle this situation and can then successfully open up opportunities for themselves, having the experiences and maturity that enable them to deal with the situation. This is not a criticism of young girls but merely a reflection of the strains of adolescence which with young men often seem to take the form of an aggressive attitude. It is the period when the extremes of masculinity and feminity are most tightly embraced. Similiar findings are reported from Sweden where efforts to introduce changes in occupational segregation found a similar clinging to roles in adolescence even when the young girls did accept that employment would play a major part in their futures:

> It was been argued that the age at which girls and boys make their educational choices, and thus for the most part their vocational decisions, is a particularly unfortunate one from the point of view of a better balance between the sexes. This is a period when young people are most anxious about establishing their identity as feminine or masculine and least likely to make choices that seem inconsistent with this image. . . . The National Labour Market Board's 'equality program' adopted in 1977 argues:

> > Sex roles are most manifest and sensitive between the ages of 14 and 25, which is a stage when a person finds it necessary to prove his or her essential capability as a man or a woman. Only when this identity has been successfully established does one feel ready to go on and become a whole person.

> > (Scott, 1982, p. 130)

All these comments suggests that not only should teachers in FE pay more attention to the way in which their courses are structured and run but that provision should be made in such a way as to attract more mature female entrants into non-traditional areas.

CHAPTER 6

Returning to Work

One further group of particular importance in relation to training policy is that of returners to work. As Chapter 2 indicated, 1 in every 2 married women now work and the female labour force now has a majority of married women. However, the fact that married women are so much in evidence means that a new pattern of work has emerged. No longer do women retire from employment upon marriage or upon childbirth, instead they are likely to be a large percentage of the labour force for much of their adult life. This in turn means that many of them have an interrupted work pattern. It is still common for many women with children to withdraw from the labour force and then return to work when their children are slightly older. Obviously this aggregate pattern varies somewhat among ethnic groups, and among local labour markets, in some places there may not be the work for women to get, so a return to work can only remain an aspiration. It is also the case that there is an increasing tendency for women to return to work when their children are still very small rather than when compulsory schooling begins – which tended to be the case in the past (Martin and Roberts, 1984). In 1971 only 20 per cent of those women with children under 5 worked, five years later in 1976 26 per cent worked (Rothwell, 1980, p. 169).

There is no official government policy in relation to women returning to work. This is not necessarily the case in other countries nor has it always been so in the past in Britain. In

91

countries where the birth rate is falling dramatically there are often pronatalist policies with financial rewards for women willing to stay in the home and nurture children. On other occasions and at different times we know that the opposite has occurred, that various government departments have been actively involved in recruiting women for work, as happened in the last war. Then women were wanted, not just in the already feminised areas of employment, but in those jobs previously held by men. Women were shipyard workers, plane manufacturers, transport drivers, male replacements in a depleted labour force. Today the Government has no such formal policy towards women and there is certainly no outward recognition of the part that women who return to work are playing in the existing labour force. Yet although there is no official policy, that does not mean that there are not elements in existence which act on and limit the opportunities open to such women. The construction of a Welfare State built on assumptions of women's dependence and the persistence of the idea of a family wage have contributed to the social attitude that regards men as being the breadwinners and the female employment and financial contribution as secondary. All this occurs despite the empirical evidence in Britain of the large number of families who would be in poverty without the female income (even where there are two wage earners) and the growing number of single-parent families, the majority of which are female-headed.

If male employment is seen as more important so too is work itself seen as male, and this, in itself, also has repercussions for women. Because men don't have similar absences from the workforce for childrearing, work and careers are seen, as occurring without such breaks, and promotion constructed on the assumption of continuing participation in the labour market. A move to another, better post is accepted but an absence from employment for the equally important task of looking after children isn't. Similarly part-time work is generally work of low status, examples of job sharing being few and far between and involving even fewer men. Yet women with family responsibilities are overwhelmingly located in part-time work. 90 per cent of all part-time workers are women, and part-timers make up 45 per cent of the female labour force (Pahl, 1984). Of these part-timers approximately 80 per cent are married. The fact that part-time work is so predominantly female, taken in conjunction with the general social attitudes that relegate female employment, helps to account for the poor manner in which part-time work is treated, with 1 million part-time workers excluded from the main provisions of employment legislation in Britain. Part-time work has come to mean low status, poorly paid, female employment and yet women continue to seek it. It's often the only solution when there are children:

> An extra hour would bring in a few extra pounds which we could use, but now I take the kids to school and collect them. That's important. The children have to come first. Besides I couldn't afford to send them by bus – that'd be £7 a week! There's nowhere they could wait from 4 till 5 – if only there was a library or a Wimpy bar even . . .
>
> (Divorcee quoted in Rothwell, 1980, p. 179)

For many women the solution will only come when part-time work itself is changed, when it has the same benefits and opportunities attached to it that full-time employment now has. The EEC is taking an interest in this area but possibly change will only really come when men too see it as an advantage that they should have part-time work. This, of course, is in tune with many feminist demands that men should take a greater role in family care and responsibilities. Considerable debate has taken place around this issue. Amongst some of the conclusions reached are a call for a convergence between part-time and full-time jobs, with shorter hours for full-timers and better conditions for part-timers, and the possibility of all parents, male and female, having an option of half-time work for a period after a child is born (Phillips, 1983).

However, changes in the actual shape of work may be some time in coming. In the meantime as part of the effort to reshape work and opportunities training can play a role. Many of the women who now return to work get jobs which are lower in status and rewards than their previous occupation. This is because they want part-time work and much of this work carries the lower pay and status. The better jobs are often not organised in such a way that they can offer part-time employment, even though in many cases, women offer the equivalent to a full-time commitment in their reduced hours. But in other cases women can end up with poorer jobs and opportunities because they lack the confidence or qualifications to their get the educational experience they need or to look to new employment horizons. In this respect training courses can help and where women are contemplating full-time employment training could be a major determinant of the level at which they re-enter the labour force. When many women's youngest child is at school by the time they are 35 this leaves a possible full-time working life of 25 years, far too many years for women to consistently face a lower horizon of opportunity and development.

For many women a major problem facing them when they want to return to work is that they don't know what they can do, what possibilities there are. They know they want to do something, but what?

> I feel very frustrated and sometimes (actually nearly all the time) very angry at many things happening in our world today, and more so because I don't feel a part of what is going on. I would like to contribute something in some way, but I don't know where or how to begin.
>
> (Quoted in Thompson, 1983, p. 49)

For some women like this adult education classes may be a first step. Throughout the country there are a variety of such classes on offer. They could be offered by the local education authorities, the WEA (Workers Education Association), or as extra-mural courses by local colleges or universities. Such courses come from a variety of sources but they often have things in common. They are sometimes seen to be about 'leisure', and the kind of topics that are taught may reflect this. Local history, literature, upholstery, gardening etc, all fit this theme although increasingly courses like women's writing or women's studies are starting to creep into the curriculum. GCE 'O' and 'A' level courses are also popular but are seen as vocational and therefore different. Adult education is the one area of education in which women outnumber men. And, unlike many other areas of educational provision, many of the teachers are also women; the part-time hours suit their family responsibilities! Jane Thompson has argued, however, that adult education not only reflects class divisions but is also deeply patriarchal, asserting male values and women's inferiority (Thompson, 1983). She sees a hierarchy in adult education, with a clear gap between the kind of extra-mural courses offered by universities, for example, and those classes run by LEAs. However, more important is the relationship between adult education and male values. She sees the very kinds of provision made in these classes, the way in which student needs are perceived and justified, as something intrinsically male and therefore as not meeting the actual needs of women.

> The 'feminine' nature of the objectives are not to women's advantage, however, because they rely on a male construction of female need, in circumstances in which men are the providers and need meeters, and women are the recipients. As with the sexual division of labour general, the adult education relationship is essentially a relationship of female tutor and students' subordination to male organisation and control. In the process, women's real needs (i.e. the definition women would make about themselves and their lives if men were not around or if men were not being recognised or met). It is not distractions that women seek, but space; not confidence, but autonomy.   (Thompson, 1983, p. 86)

From this perspective what the majority of women are offered in adult education will only serve to help women to adjust to an existing world, a world in which they are already severely disadvantaged, rather than give them the opportunities to develop in ways which will help them transform this situation. However, the introduction of courses such as women's studies could help to alleviate this situation, offering women a critical perspective on their world. Nor need the view of existing provision be entirely negative. For some women adult education courses can be a stepping-stone, a first step towards other courses, a way of opening out.

For women who look to educational provision as a way of qualifying them on the labour market there are many different

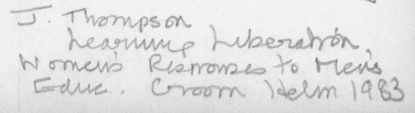

J. Thompson
Learning Liberation,
Women's Responses to Men's
Educ. Croom Helm 1983

kinds of provision. Some can go directly to colleges or universities as mature students. In the majority of cases the formal educational requirements are waived for mature students. For those who have neither the time or the opportunity to go to existing higher education institutions the Open University offers a way to earn a degree in the students' own time and locality, using radio, television and cassette provision to supplement written course units (the equivalent of lectures), as well as calling on local resource centres and locally based tutors. The Open University has offered many women the educational experience they thought they had missed. For some the Open University is a way of opening up new career prospects. Others have gained promotion through their studies in the university. The success rate for women studying with the Open University is high, higher than that of men, in fact, but there is still a tendency for women to register more in the Arts and Social Sciences Faculties than in the scientific and technical areas, though the numbers in the latter are constantly rising (Griffiths, 1980).

However, for many women the idea of taking a degree can be too much to contemplate at first. For women who feel this a wide variety of courses are available, although their provision is somewhat scattered and unplanned. Such courses could offer the opportunity to return to study or they could be providing opportunities that are more along the lines of a return to work – although both can, in practice, be dealing with areas of education. The return to study courses appear under titles like 'Fresh Horizons', 'Return to Study' or 'Foundation Courses'. They are open to both men or women unless specifically designated under Clause 47 of the Sex Discrimination Act, but in many cases they are populated by a majority of women. Such courses, either full-time or part-time, offer a road into further levels of education, but it has been argued that women are not in a position to benefit from them on equal terms with men, mainly because of the intense pressures on many of them in their family relationships. As one study of the participants in a Fresh Horizons course found:

> Types of domestic pressure ranged from blatant hostility to a subtle, more insidious, sort of psychological pressure which

amounted to 'sabotage'. Middle-class and working-class women faced criticism from home but the tactics of the middle classes proved harder to deal with and were more effective academic deterrents than the frank working-class disapproval. Middle-class women were subjected to simultaneous, contradictory messages which patted them on the head for being clever girls but sent out warnings if the work was taken too seriously. The studying was OK so long as it did not threaten the status quo and would be dropped wherever it did.

(Lovell, 1980, p. 221)

The point is that women do go on into further and higher education from these courses but they are at a disadvantage compared to male participants in such programmes.

Other courses are more specifically geared to a return to work. They aim to offer women who are thinking of returning to the labour market the confidence and experiences that will help them choose an area of work, often new to them, and get a job. Again these courses are fairly widely scattered over the country and it is unclear just how many there are. They are also referred to by a variety of names: New Opportunities for Women' (NOW), 'Return to Work', 'Fresh Horizons', or 'Wider Opportunities for Women' (WOW). The courses are usually short in duration, part-time and no formal qualifications are required, but conditions can very widely from area to area. Most of the courses, however, are based on a desire to help women make the transition into the labour market and stress guidance and counselling aimed at increasing the confidence of women, many of whom are reassured by discovering other women with the same problems and doubts. Such is the impact and morale-raising effect of the courses that many participants decide to go on into further education rather than employment, once they develop the confidence that makes them feel such a stretching-out is possible. In other cases participation in the course gives women the confidence to take up opportunities that were already open to them but which they had never taken up. Participants in a NOW scheme at Hatfield, for instance, experienced all these effects. Mrs B became the clinic supervisor of a Family Planning clinic after the course and said:

> I had been a voluntary worker with FPA for several years. During this time the paid position of supervisor had become vacant more than once but I never applied for it, partly through lack of confidence. I think the course restored my confidence. (Michaels, 1973, p. 21)

Another woman, Mrs D, started to think about teacher training:

> it gave me a terrific boost in self-confidence. After talking to the college counsellor I gained the confidence to actually apply for admission to college. The self-confidence held in spite of being rejected by two colleges and it still holds.
> (Michaels, 1973, p. 22)

Despite the very obvious impact that the courses have for many women there remain problems. The most obvious is, of course, their patchy provision. Women who might want such a course could easily find there are none in their part of the country especially in rural areas. Where courses are provided, creches and suitable hours for collecting school-going children are also a necessity. In many cases these needs are being met, although the timetabling to match with school hours still seems a problem in many cases (Stoney and Reid, 1981). These provisions are a necessity. Stoney and Reid, in their study of further opportunities for women identified child care and timetabling as the key factors in encouraging women back into courses (1980, p. 37). Another problem is that of effectively reaching the target population for such courses and easing entry. In many cases advertising of the courses is in newspapers or in the prospectuses of colleges, both sources of information that many women may not encounter, unlike notices posted in areas they may frequent more often, such as supermarkets, child health centres or community centres.

Many of the NOW courses and their equivalents are to be found in colleges where they are often the result of the enthusiasm of particular tutors. However, the MSC has organised similar courses called Wider Opportunities for Women (WOW) which are designed, administered and financed by the Training Services Division of the MSC, although they too are to be found inside colleges. The MSC courses are aimed at

Stoney & Reid
Further Opps in Focus (1981
FEU Unit London

women who are likely to enter manual or skilled employment and although participants can be as young as 19 the courses have tended to attract older women. As in the college courses the MSC courses aim to provide women with information and self-confidence which will help them both formulate realistic re-entry plans and carry them out.

The courses can be full-time or part-time, lasting six to twelve weeks, and women on the courses pay no fees but can, as well, receive a training allowance. In content NOW and WOW courses can be similar, offering information, discussion and counselling and an assessment of local employment opportunities. In WOW courses there is also job sampling with students having the opportunity to sample two jobs out of four job clusters. Often these are traditional female occupations but the sampling can also, on occasions, provide access to jobs such as welding or bricklaying. These courses started on an experimental basis in 1979 and have undergone a modest expansion. They are now run in about 20 centres and in 1983/4 572 places were being offered, a fairly small dent in the national demand (there were also about 93 places for women returning to management or entering new technology jobs). These figures reflect a small commitment to women returners.

As well as the WOW courses aimed specifically at female returners to work the MSC also provides opportunities through the Training Opportunities Scheme (TOPS). The TOPS programmes were not set up for school leavers but were aimed at those who were at least 19 and had been out of permanent education for at least two years. Both men and women were eligible for the courses and the number of women participants has gradually grown. In 1972 only 6,000 women trained on TOPS programmes but by 1975 it was 27,000 and by 1978 the number was about 41,000 so that by 1980 women made up nearly half of those on the TOPS schemes. Obviously women were attracted to TOPS but once again the gender stereotyping seen in the youth programmes of the MSC is also in evidence. Women predominate in the programmes dealing with shothand, typing and clerical work and are also in a majority on those courses dealing with food preparation, cleaning, hairdressing etc., that is all those areas where women predominate in paid employment.

Despite the fact that many women are using the schemes there are still many restraints on others who might otherwise find the programmes attractive. This is particularly so in relation to women who are returning to work. As in so many other instances there are problems relating to childcare and to the structure of the programmes, the majority of which are full-time and therefore do not relate to the existing structure of many womens days. The failure to provide childcare and more flexible timing in relation to the programmes has been defended by members of the MSC on occasion. It is felt that if women want to enter the labour market they will not find creches or convenient hours waiting for them there and so they should adjust from the start. As Sir Richard O'Brien, then chairman of the Manpower Services Commission, wrote in a letter in December, 1981:

> We consider it is important that applicants for training should demonstrate that they can make arrangements to cope with domestic commitments during the course of their training as they will have to do so if they wish to take employment.

Even where MSC staff recognise that childcare could be important there is evidence that this commitment does not stretch to having MSC money put into providing such facilities, as in the Deptford skill centre. Deptford, in London, got the first childcare facility in any government skill centre only after they were promised funding by local councils, the MSC having consistently refused to provide finance. Yet if childcare facilities aren't provided the fact that the training allowance for TOPS courses is small becomes important because it will be difficult to arrange for private childcare from this sum. As well as the mainstream TOPS courses there is also a small programme of experimental courses for women provided through TOPS. These include returners courses, some of which are related to new technology or to management but the numbers are also small. There were about 450 women on these courses in 1983/4 (WNC Conference, 1984).

Some women do try and use the TOPS courses to enter areas where male workers predominate, especially manual jobs. Even when these women have confidence and experience of the area they wish to enter, access to the courses is not straightforward as the following experience illustrates:

> The first stage of a TOPS application takes place in the job centre. The man who was dealing with my application obviously had some aspirations in the area of careers counselling. He seemed to feel that because I had stayed on at school I was suited to a 'better' job. I argued with him that I was not seeking status but job satisfaction; that I hated office work, and felt that joinery required quite a lot of intelligence anyway. He went out of his way to impress on me that joinery was not putting shelves up, but mostly very heavy work including a lot of work at heights (this is a very inaccurate description of the trade). He was also very conscientious about saving the taxpayers' money, on the one hand being suspicious that I was only doing the course in order to do my own house up and sell it for more money; on the other hand he was confident that no one would employ me as a joiner so it would be a waste of money training me.
>
> (At the interview, the next stage in the application:) The interview was a reflection of their attitudes towards women, which ranged from hostile to bemused. They thought it was definitely not a good idea that I should go on the course . . . I was not strong enough; I would not get a job afterwards; there were no toilet facilities for women; women could only lift heavy things like handbags; if I used the men's toilets I might get raped. They spent a lot of time questioning each other over what could be done with me . . . 'Perhaps plumbing would be better?' 'Oh no, she would have to carry a bath upstairs on her own!' It was very hard to know how to react to all this, (R. Ardron, *WEPG Newsletter*, No. 1)

For many women the reaction would be all too clear, they would be discouraged and alienated. Yet it is unlikely that such experiences are exceptional and it certainly helps explain the very small numbers of women who do make in onto TOPS courses.

The courses outlined above offer a wide variety of experiences and require different attributes and commitment on the part of participants. They vary, also, in ease of access to schemes and the practical problems that have to be overcome if many women are to take advantage of these opportunities.

What the schemes have in common, though is the fact that they take place outside the labour market. They may prepare women for re-entry, open their eyes to educational possibilities or job opportunities, albeit often in 'feminised' areas, but they do not provide a path directly into employment. For many women this must be an important lack for although some may welcome the opportunity to change direction or employer others may well feel that they are missing a lot by not being able to return to their own old firm or position. Whilst maternity leave legislation now extends job protection to many women, allowing them to return to their own employment positions a short time after their children are born, such protection is not extended on into the early years of child-rearing and many women do want to share these years with their children. Yet, is such a possibility more than a pipe dream?

In Sweden social policy legislation gives parents an opportunity to preserve their jobs yet still spend far more extensive periods of time with their small children. Here, in Britain, one or two firms are gradually realising that female workers represent an investment that they should not so easily toss away and are starting to introduce re-entry schemes. One such business organisation is the National Westminster Bank which has introduced a re-entry and reservist scheme. This scheme, introduced for an experimental five-year period in 1981, allows employees an extended career break. Although the break extends to both men and women, it seems likely that in current circumstances it would be of great interest to women. The two schemes are in operation for a period of five years from the date of resignation at the expiry of state maternity leave. The first scheme, the re-entry scheme, is open to those who have the potential for senior management positions and allows an individual to re-enter at the same level and grade as when they left. For the reserve scheme participants have to have the potential to reach junior/middle management and for them re-employment is not guaranteed, but they will be considered for suitable vacancies at the level or grade they occupied previously. Both groups have to undertake at least two weeks paid relief work a year and attend an annual seminar. They are also encouraged to continue with the Institute of Banking examinations. Selection for the scheme is by the bank.

In light of the discussion of the discussion of banking in Chapter 5 there are drawbacks to this scheme that one would not want if such initiatives were to become more general. It was clear from the evidence presented there that many women, often because of discrimination by male bank officials, have not been gaining access to promotion ladders. In such circumstances a scheme revolving around selection by the bank itself and only involving those small numbers that have made it onto the managerial ladder cannot be a scheme that can benefit many. On the other hand, it is gratifying to see any attempt by employers that would give women returners access to the grades, salary and promotional ladder they had when they gave up work for childcare.

This example does, however, suggest the optimistic conclusion that a lot more could be done to ensure the re-entry of women into excellent jobs. Where one employer can do it so can others. On the other hand, it also shows how easily limited such schemes are to those few women a step or more up the promotional ladder, when other women could also benefit from such arrangements.

It is also possible, although comparatively rare, for women to re-enter the field of employment at a substantially different level and in a different field to those they left. One way in which this can be done is through training for management courses. These are not yet common but there is an increasing realisation that there are vast numbers of women, a potential pool of talent, awaiting such opportunities. One recent course at Gloucester College of Arts and Technology had several hundred applicants for a course that could offer only fifteen places (Patritti-Jagger, 1983). Such course can tap previous work experiences but also those other experiences which women have and which are often overlooked:

> As well as the care of my children I had spent a lot of time actively involved in voluntary work. Ten years were devoted to Liberal politics in Surrey including three years as District Councillor. I also acted as agent in both General Elections in 1974. My experience has included being the chairman of

several groups and organising fund raising activities and I am currently a school governor, a prison visitor and a member of a Parochial Church Council and Deanery Synod. I have always enjoyed the responsibility of planning, organising and managing. (J. Harber, member of the Women into Management Course, 1983)

Industry training Boards, recently drastically reduced in number by the Thatcher Government, are also very supportive of efforts to get women into management, but ITB's in areas like clothing, which are female-dominated, experience considerable resistance to the promotion of women within jobs let alone in those returning to work. The Food, Drink and Tobacco ITB, however, introduced a small number (20) of grants for companies which employed or trained women as managers or supervisors following a work break for domestic reasons of over five years (Rothwell, 1980, p. 197).

In the majority of cases those employers, still few in number, who do provide retraining are only interested in those women who have already made substantial progress within the company. Few indeed are prepared to recognise that at least some of the women now looking for employment once their children are older will now have developed aspirations and the desire to do something more than dead-end work.

CHAPTER 7

Comparative Perspectives

In the 1970s the advent of the Equal Pay Act and the Sex Discrimination Act in Britain seemed to offer hope that an era of equal opportunities was opening, and that old patterns of discrimination would disappear. Legislation was equated with actual social change. In the 1980s it has become clear that legislation, at least in Britain, has not produced much change. The legislation embodies a notion of equality, but the reality is that women's opportunities are still restricted and that the gap between men and women in terms of pay is getting wider rather than narrower (Robarts, 1981). Examination of all the different areas of training has quite clearly shown that substantive differences still exist between men and women in terms of the training opportunities and therefore the job and career prospects open to them. If the legislation is such a failure in terms of making any marked difference in the relative positions of men and women, does this mean that any legislative attempt to alter gender divisions in society will fail, *or* that the problem lies with the kind of legislation that Britain has?

The question can be asked because it's clear that other countries have tried to tackle the same problems in different ways. It is worth comparing what has happened in Britain with countries such as the USA which have a markedly different type of legislation, with Sweden where a wide variety of techniques addressing gender divisions in society have been utilised, and with Eastern Europe where a society with a different economic base often seems to present a different picture of the role of women.

In Britain the Sex Discrimination Act (SDA) is seen as a negative form of legislation; this is particularly so when compared to the 'positive' elements of the American legislative experience (Robarts, 1981). It is termed negative in that it tries to prohibit the worst forms of discrimination and unequal treatment between the sexes, but it is not seen as having had any real impact on the basic gender divisions in society. Many commentators feel that such a negative approach is necessarily doomed to failure, that such divisions will only respond to legislation that takes an active and positive role in removing disadvantages. As it stands the British legislation remains 'one of the most significant achievments of the 1970s and one which affects most women's lives hardly at all' (Coyle, 1984, p. 138).

The existing legislation has many failings. One major part of the problem with existing legislation is that cases under the SDA can only be brought by individuals. If the case is won, its outcome only affects that particular individual. So if Ms Jones, for example, wins a case which says she is being unlawfully blocked off from training opportunities in her firm, that decision and case only affects her, and Ms Smith sitting next to her in the same office will have to take her own case to prove that she too is having her career prospects blighted in the same way. In the USA by comparison, it is possible to take cases that involve groups, or classes of individuals, not just one person; this, of course, gives decisions taken in court a much wider importance. Furthermore in Britain the burden of proof is on the complainant. Discrimination is so often through attitudes that any formal kind of evidence is difficult to muster. When a complaint is made the individual making the complaint will often find that the employer or institution being complained about has access to expert advice and legal assistance that can help formulate an effective defence. The complainant, on the other hand, will probably be unable to muster such expert assistance, unless she has union membership and the union is supporting the case and providing the suitably qualified expertise. Such support is not, however, necessarily a consequence of union membership. If unions have been ambivalent about the development of legislation and the activities of the EOC, there is also evidence available suggesting that they can be far from helpful when women workers attempt to use the equality legislation that does exist. On occasion unions seem to share more with management (male) in respect to this than they do with the workers they represent (female). One study found that:

> Many union representatives shared management's assumptions that there was no need for action, either because they also believed women had equal opportunity or because they were hostile to the idea and consequences of equal opportunity . . . Union representatives in one organisation dismissed women's complaints of discrimination with the statement that it was 'management's right to select whoever they liked'.
>
> (Snell, 1979)

It is perhaps ironic in light of the evidence in earlier chapters that one of the few areas in which the existing British legislation allows positive discrimination is that of training. The Manpower Services Commission, the Training Services Division and the Employment Services Agency as well as the Industrial Training Boards – such as the Engineering Board – are allowed to take positive action in certain circumstances; so too are employers. These provisions are meant to work for the benefit of women. Where a particular occupation has been done mainly or exclusively by men over the last twelve months, an employer can encourage women to do that work and provide them with the training that is necessary. Similar opportunities are available to training bodies. In the same situation they can encourage women into these areas by providing women-only training or limiting access to training to women. This can be done at a national level or in one particular area of the country where there is an imbalance. The fact that so little has so far been achieved in the one area where positive action is allowed illustrates even further the inadequacies of existing legislation.

In the USA, on the other hand, the development of legislation does seem to have made some difference in terms of opportunity. This can only be because the whole legislation was envisaged in terms of positive action and because subsequent changes and developments have strengthened and developed the activities of the Equal Employment Opportunity Commission. That is not to say that the situation is in any way perfect: far from it. The general picture is still far from satisfactory. There is still strong occupational segregation, and women still earn a much lower figure than the average male wage, around 60–70 per cent, according to profession. Yet there have been some major improvements at a different level, mainly within large corporations which have begun to take equality legislation seriously. Their response has often been triggered by the activities of the Equal Employment Opportunities Commission (EEOC) which has been prepared to take action against some of the corporate giants including the Bank of America and AT&T (The American Telephone and Telegraph Company) – the world's largest corporation.

The legislation that deals with positive action in the USA was not, however, developed specifically to deal with gender divisions in society. Instead, the legislation was a response to the much wider question of civil rights. It is Title VII of the Civil Rights Act of 1964 that bans sex discrimination in employment. The EEOC was set up under this title but at first could only look for voluntary compliance with the act. The EEOC could, however, file *amicus curiae* briefs and guidelines which are thought to have had a 'significant' influence on the law (Meehan, 1983, p. 178). After 1972 the EEOC was able to litigate and could therefore take bodies to court either in individual cases or in 'class' or group actions. The effect of the legislation was widened by the issue of Executive Orders. These orders by the President have immense effects. One order, for instance (No. 11246), forbade all government departments and all employers with substantial government contracts from discriminating against ethnic minorities, and in a subsequent order (No. 11375) this was widened to include discrimination on the grounds of sex. Later orders specified in detail the ways employers had to behave in order to comply with the original orders (Robarts, 1981, pp. 23–25). Central to the scheme is the proposition that all local labour markets and their own organisations have to be analysed by the firms involved, and that if an organisation employs smaller numbers of women and minorities than are available from the local market then the organisation has to develop an affirmative action programme. Such a programme has to contain both goals and timetables, that is numbers and dates.

These legislative developments seem to offer hope to women and ethnic minorities and many corporations have put affirmative action programmes into operation. Many of these firms have done so voluntarily, others such as AT&T did so after action by the EEOC. On an individual basis such programmes do seem to be transforming opportunities for women. In General Motors, for instance, the affirmative action programme resulted in a rise in the proportion of women students in the engineering college from 0.6 per cent in 1970 to 32 per cent in 1977 (Robarts, 1981, p. 41). Yet as Sadie Robarts points out, the overall picture is still fairly bleak in the USA. Although women are nearly half the labour force they are still in 'feminised' occupational ghettoes overall, still at lower levels, and still with far lower rates of pay. And, as Robarts also demonstrates, many of the changes that have occurred can be merely cosmetic ones. Firms can appear to have met the equality criterion but in fact have only re-defined jobs – renaming them but without changing either the job itself or the salary. Other employers may promote more women, for example, or employ more, but will segregate them within the organisation so that a gender-segregated pattern of employment continues, but this time hidden inside the aggregate figures for employees presented by that organisation. In other cases the affirmative action programme itself is weak. Robarts suggests that there are many lessons to be learnt from the American experience if we are to have effective positive action programmes. The first of these is that it is necessary to have clear statistical data about actual and potential members of the workforce if realistic objectives are to be set up. The programmes themselves have to be drawn up in detail and all the possible blocks to initial entry and continued participation catered for. Vital to the success of any scheme seems to be the commitment of employees. This means that avoidance strategies by employers would be a thing of the past but also that members of an organisation, at all levels, would be committed to the goal of the affirmative action programme. The importance of this and the necessity of training participants at all levels to see that this is so is clearly illustrated earlier in the discussion of internal labour markets within organisations. There it was clear that many of the most substantial blocks to women's advance lay in the attitudes of many of their superiors, who consciously or unconsciously were not prepared to train women for promotion and development. Another central element in any such programme would also be the existence of an effective evaluation and monitoring system. Only then could a programme be adjusted to deal with any failings that show up as the programme runs.

All this, of course, assumes that an effective programme could be run. It is based on a belief that attitudes *can* be changed and that effective evaluation and reaction can help to overcome any resistance inherent within members of the organisation. Yet evidence from other countries continues to raise doubts about how far positive action programmes can be effective. A comparative perspective continues to present a pessimistic picture of the situation of women, even when political ideologies are firmly in support of such changes.

One of the countries most often pointed to as having altered the role of women at work is the USSR. Pictures of female road-sweepers, of female building workers, engineers or even astronauts are known to decorate books and articles on the Soviet Union. The fact that there are greater percentages of female engineers or female doctors than in the West seems at first glance to indicate a different kind of society with different roles for women and far more occupational opportunities. A closer examination reveals, however, just how superficial such a picture is. Occupational segregation by gender, both vertical and horizontal, in the levels of work and the kinds of work, is just as prevalent in the East as it is in the West. There may be more doctors who are women – they make up 75 per cent of all doctors and dentists in Russia – but they remain in the jobs with less status or authority. Similarly 44 per cent of engineers and technicians are female, but they too don't get into management or administrative jobs in number proportionale to their presence in those occupations (Lapidus, 1978). Yet the USSR is a country that has always had women's equality as a major political goal. The government has consistently encouraged the entry of women into the labour force and the massive numbers of men killed in the Second World War made female labour a necessity. For many women there are also financial pressures to push them out into the labour market. Over 85 per cent of all women aged between 25 and 55 are employed full-time in industry and agriculture but despite the importance of their participation in relation to the economy inequalities based on gender remain. Indeed, one commentator has argued it is the very fact that economic growth rather than equality is the goal that has allowed these inequalities to be continually reproduced (Jancar, 1981). Gender stereotyping of jobs remains as prevalent as in the West; it is merely the occupations that are characterised as 'male' or 'female' that differ slightly. Within them women are found at the same low level. In agriculture, for instance, where women predominate as they do in all Eastern European countries, female workers are found in the areas of low status and pay. They are the ones to be found milking by hand rather than driving the tractors, looking after the poultry rather than administering the farm (Lapidus, 1978, p. 179). In industry the same pattern is clear. In the low skill categories women predominate over men in a ratio of 5 to 1, yet in the three highest skill categories the situation is exactly the reverse: men outnumber women, five to one. As one Russian woman sees it:

> In the Soviet Union it is taken for granted that women will work on railroad beds, on road crews, on construction sites and as janitors or cleaning ladies . . . On collective and state farms, women do the hardest and most exhausting work while the men are employed as administrators, agronomists, accountants, warehouse managers, or high-paid tractor and combine drivers. In other words, men do the work that is more interesting and profitable and does not damange their health.
>
> (Mamanova, 1984, pp. 7–8)

The situation of women in the Soviet Union is similar to that of women in the West in many other ways. They too are worn

out and constrained by the demands of their role within the
family. Inadequate housing and childcare do not make their
role in employment any easier and they too are faced with
entrenched masculine attitudes which assign the responsibility
for home and childcare to them. Is this a description of life
for many a working woman in Moscow or in London, in
Birmingham or in Leningrad?

> Tired after their workday, they hurry home to childcare
> centres. Bowed with the weight of grocery bags, they drag
> their children behind them. In a terrible crush of people, they
> wedge themselves into overcrowded public buses elbowing
> people aside and pushing their way to an empty seat if there is
> one. At last they reach home, new cares await them. Dinner
> must be prepared and the husband and children fed. The
> laundry and the housecleaning still wait.
>
> (Golubeva, 1984, p. 27)

In many ways the situation in the Soviet Union appears
worse than that in the West as far as women are concerned.
The problems of economic development still pose a major
headache for the Soviet government and it seems that this will
remain their priority to the detriment of the goal of gender
equality. Although the government tried to open up higher
education opportunities for women, recognising that lack of
such educational opportunities posed an obstacle to the
advancement of women in general, it remains a fact that after
entry gender stereotyping once again occurs and women spe-
cialise in educational areas such as health care, education and
accounting. Furthermore, the Soviet Union appears to be a
deeply misogynist society with entrenched anti-feminist social
attitudes. The rise of any feminist movement has been
regarded with hostility by the authorities, including possible
physical coercion (Mamonova, 1984). It it this situation which
has led at least one commentator to the belief that the future
for Soviet women is bleak:

> any genuine radical departures in female roles and status and
> in male female relationships and authority patterns more
> broadly in the years ahead are far more likely to take place in
> some western societies than in the USSR
>
> (Lapidus, 1978, p. 346)

If it's necessary to look to the West for the possible end of major gender divisions in society then such changes seem most likely to occur in Sweden, the one European country that has undertaken a major sex equality programme aimed at all areas of life. Led mainly by the SDP (the Social Democratic Party) the government in Sweden has used its powers over the last twenty years to try and achieve equality between the sexes. In doing so it has aimed to eliminate sex discrimination, to establish labour market and education policies that would counter sex determined choices, and to provide an infrastructure of expanded services, especially in the areas of childcare and transport, that would allow these first goals to be achieved.

The ability of a government to introduce a programme with such far-reaching aims is rooted in the Swedish commitment to a coherent, and consistent social policy that has developed historically:

> Swedes became used to the idea that social policies, to be effective, cannot be applied individually, like band-aids or the legendary finger in the dike, but must be part of a consistent programme. (Scott, 1982, p. 12)

While state social policies in Britain are often convoluted and not infrequently contradictory, with one area of government going one way and a different department another, Swedish social policy attempts to provide a unitary system so that education, childcare provision, transport, health, social welfare, industrial and regional policies are all attuned to the same goal.

Central to developments in Sweden has been the recognition that the goal of achieving equality between the sexes means changing the role of men as much as changing the role of women. The ultimate objective was a non-sexist society in which men and women would have the same options, the same opportunities and the same obligations. However, the situation that the Swedes faced when they formulated this goal was not dissimiliar to the one that existed in many other Western societies. Occupations were gender-segregated, female earnings were lower and many women made up a substantial number of the poor in Swedish society. Women were responsible for the home and family and many preferred part-time work because of this situation.

Attempts to change this situation were wide-ranging. There already existed a powerful machine for initiating activity in the area of training and employment. This was the National Labour Market Board whose job was to maintain full employment through placements, but which could also, if necessary, initiate public works and give government contracts to prevent lay-offs or shutdowns. As part of its task it also organised training and supervised training within firms with the use of government subsidies. It also had an investment fund to promote further enterprises or expansion. The tradition therefore already existed of a state agency based on co-operation from both sides of industry which took an active part in manipulating the labour market. Moves to change the employment structures and prospects for men and women were therefore based on a system of direction that was already well accepted. On the other hand until 1979 there was no legislation forbidding discrimination on the basis of sex, mainly because the unions wished to maintain their tradition of reaching voluntary rather than legislative solutions. One important experiment that took place in the early 1970 and which was later spread to other regions by the National Labour Market Board was the Kristianstad programme. This was a project which aimed to recruit women workers into 'male' industries in a region that was experiencing labour shortages. The national effect was far-reaching:

> If there was anyone in those years in Sweden who did not know what Kristianstad meant, it could only have been because they did not read papers or watch TV. The young women who managed to handle heavy insulator parts without damaging them and to glaze washbasins and lift them on a conveyor belt, and the bulky workmates who said that at first they had been dubious but had discovered women could (or sometimes could not) do their share were good for endless human interest stories. Television programmes turned up instructive examples of sexism on the part of interviewers as well as interviewees. Kristianstad brought real life from the factory floor into the discussions that climaxed in International Women's Year.　　　　　(Scott, 1982, p. 28)

One of the problems that rose out of the whole debate and one that is still very contemporary was what kind of occupations women should move into. In other words were men's jobs *per se* to be the goal? Whilst many male jobs undoubtedly offered more variety, more responsibility and the possibility of promotion there were also many other male jobs that were low-level, which required little skill and could be hazardous and dangerous. Why should women wish to move into these occupations? Do men accept them only because it is 'manly' to do so? The desire of many women to work part-time and to have time with their children had also to be respected. Why should everyone have, or want, to work full-time? The questions that women's advancement raised were also questions about the nature and form of work, questions that were equally applicable to men. Did they, too, not want safer jobs, cleaner jobs, time with their children?

Divisions in the labour market were seen to be related, as in other countries, to the sex divisions that developed in the course of schooling. Many changes were initiated in the education system in the 1960s and 70s. The first round of changes aimed to produce a unitary system as part of a process of democratisation, and directives as early as 1969 called for efforts to ensure a free choice of study and career and to question the sex differences that had become established. Both groups were to be made aware that the root of much segregation and discrimination lay in unequal shares in childcare and home chores, and domestic science and childcare were made compulsory subjects for both sexes. Yet as one sex-role project found some changes were easier to achieve than others.

> Every girl now thinks in terms of a job. This is progress. They want children, but they don't pin their hopes on marriage, They don't intend to be housewives for some future husband. But there has been no change in their vocational choices.
>
> (Scott, 1982, p. 125)

The results of studies like this led to a further round of educational changes at the end of the 1970s with an emphasis upon vocational orientation but there appear to be signs that gender roles are not getting increased attention, although it is still too early to be sure. One explanation that has been put forward to account for the lack of impact on gender stereotyping in study and occupation is the fact that the labour market has still not changed dramatically. Women know that many non-traditional job opportunities are not open to them although, in the pattern common to other European countries, males are moving into female traditional areas. Despite the efforts of the Labour Market Board and the projects discussed earlier there is still strong gender stereotyping at work. Men have not been successfully persuaded to reform their lives, and the state has not succeeded in marking career, family and childcare choices the same for men and women.

Changes have occurred in Sweden, but they have not been sufficient to achieve the kind of non-sexist society that was the goal. Once again, as in Russia, but this time in a totally different social and political structure, it is male attitudes that have been isolated as the main block to change. The Swedish vision of a new society required changes by men, changes that would touch their very hearts and consciousnesses and it is this sort of transformation that is missing. This is how Hilda Scott sees the situation in her analysis of Sweden:

> men feel that they have 'done a great deal for women' and are probably going to do a great deal more, but they expect it all to be done in the framework of existing male institutions. General precepts about men's right to be loving are fine, but challenges that go to the very essence of male ordered society – that's hitting below the belt.   (Scott, 1982, p. 158)

What she saw and what many women in Sweden have come to see is a situation where men and their value system are the main problem. Yet because so many of those men say that they support equality, resisting this powerful value system becomes more difficult than in many other societies. Women in Sweden are being 'devoured by equality'. The actual reforms that were introduced in Sweden, the changes in social policy, in industrial strategies, things only dreamt of elsewhere helped to reveal the strength of more fundamental and powerful forces in Swedish society. The 'reasonableness' of the politicians, mainly male, served only to veil the resistance of social structures, organisations and attitudes that were built on a conception of masculinity which included the continued subordination of women. In Sweden men need to change themselves and the gap between public and private in male attitudes illustrates the problem only too well. Rita Liljestrom found at Kristianstad that employers were willing to talk to researchers about their commitment to the notion of equality in the workplace, but that when asked more subtly about their own private lives and their attitude to the employment of their own wives and daughters the underlying resistance to any such moves came out strongly.

What the evidence from all these countries suggests is that legislation by itself does not work if the goal is one of removing gender differences in society. In none of the countries examined here, East or West, does any real equality exist between men and women. Even where legislation is strongest and where the political will to implement the legislation appears to be there, as in Sweden, there are problems. How much more likely is it that there will be problems in implementing any similar legislation in Britain? Here the political will is far weaker, and, as we have seen, unions, governments, employers and the Civil Service have all displayed a visible embivalence about dealing with existing sex roles in our society and the consequent discrimination against women.

What a comparative perspective shows us is the entrenched nature of male power in these societies. What is at stake is not just attitudes, but a situation in which the material interest of men acts against any gendered social change. For many feminists the problem has always been the problem of men. They search for a matriarchal past or look to a female utopia. Yet the question of male interests is more than one of 'gut reaction'. Increasingly, empirical work, undertaken in the analysis of many aspects of our society, is being forced to reach the same conclusions, to see gender divisions rather than class as the major social division in our society, a division that runs through all aspects of our lives. Research findings consistently draw attention to the way our society, our conceptions of what is public and what's private, even our political institutions as well as our social lives, are rooted in a system of male power.

The demands that women are making are not 'women's demands' but demands that require reformulation of the roles of both men and women. But as the Swedish experience shows, men are, in the end, not inclined to make these changes. They already occupy a system that presents them with material rewards although to obtain these they have to accept the prevailing definition of masculinity. Women's demands, when they are thought through, would challenge such a definition and therefore men are more than willing to ignore such issues when they can or to corral them into separate conferences, seperate agendas. While prevailing definitions survive women will continue to be seen in terms of the home and the family, the private domestic arena, cut off from the public world of men and therefore invisible even in their presence there. Men benefit from women's work within the home and use the ideology that their role is in the home to improve and sustain their own privileged position in the employment field. What changes in women's position in society entails are changes for men to, but men perceive these as a threat because of this material base, rather than as changes which would offer benefits to men as well – as Hilda Scott terms it the 'right to be human' rather than 'male'.

So where does this leave us in terms of legislation, in terms of changes? It seems certain that opportunities will not open to women of their own accord. Too much is at stake. Nor, if and when we get rid of gender divisions in society, is this likely to be a cataclysmic event, a storming of the Bastille or an attack on the Winter Palace. It seems likely that change will only come about after struggle on many fronts and that legislation has a part to play in this. As the example of the USA shows when legislation is introduced some things do get moving. In Sweden too the situation did not remain static, it just did not achieve all that women first hoped. Legislation therefore is of value, but it has also to be recognised that it is not the sole solution. In training, as in other areas of our society, more will be needed than mere Acts of Parliament. Yet even the first and most tentative steps, opposed as they are at many levels, bring immediate openings and opportunities to many women, and this is something of value that we cannot ignore.

CHAPTER 8

Extending Women's Opportunities

For many people there is not really a problem about training in relation to women; the problem is one of schooling or of the labour market. The schools are pinpointed as an explanation of the unequal position of women in the labour market because it is seen, as indeed does happen, that in the schools girls are usually not given access to many of the technical skills and subjects that would equip them for entry into many forms of training and a lot of occupations, mainly the scientific and technical ones. There is indeed sexism in our schools and numerous studies are now documenting the diverse ways in which women have been taught over the years to have different views of their role in life, to focus on the family and to see many subjects as gender-specific. The curriculum, books, teaching methods, interaction in the classroom, all of these have come to be shown to have a significant impact on the outcome of schooling for boys and girls and play an important part in the formation of gender roles. All this leads to the conclusion that substantive changes have to be made in experiences at school if the position of women and their labour market opportunities are to be transformed. Somehow the experience of schooling has to be one which doesn't contribute to the continued inequality of women in society. This, it is presumed, is what is necessary if women are to get access to the forms of training from which their current educational experience now excludes them due to lack of suitable qualifications, confidence, and so on.

For those who place on emphasis on the structure of the labour market the solution comes at the other end of the training experience, at the point of entry into paid employment. Even if women did get training, it is argued, they would not be able to get jobs because employers would not wish to take them on. Undoubtedly this is still true of many employers. Earlier chapters have documented the numerous pitfalls that women face from employers in their fight for training facilities and opportunities and for entry into career paths and promotion. Somehow the attitude of these employers has to be changed if women are to get ahead; and a more structural version of this argument suggests this is unlikely whilst so many employers profit through the low wages and limited social benefits that many women are paid.

From both these points of view training is not the main problem and therefore not the area most in urgent need of change. This does not mean to say, however, that training for women is regarded as perfect: the faults are too glaringly obvious for this. What it does mean is that other changes are assumed to come first or to have priority. Yet need this be so? Why should the training provision for women not be constructed in such a way as to both compensate for the inadequacies of the schooling process in relation to women, and also help constitute new opportunities on the labour market. Such provision does not yet exist but what might it be possible to do?

It is certainly not impossible to envisage a system where the inadequacies of schooling are compensated for rather than regarded as an experience which firmly closes the door in many women's faces. Maths, science, technical subjects, whatever it is that women have not got which is required for some forms of training, could be provided as part of the training process, a preparation for the more technical parts which at present constitute training. It is a question of finding an alternative way of providing those facilities or qualifications that women might need and which schools, at present, are not giving. In short, rather than regard the period of schooling, as too often happens, as the main point at which such facilities and diplomas are acquired, we should see it merely as one experience whose failings can be compensated for later.

Similarly, the construction of training experiences need not be so divorced from the labour market as it is, especially where government finance is involved. In Sweden, for example, loans for industrial development in the regions have been linked to the provision of training and employment opportunities for women in formerly male-dominated occupations. This could easily be done here. The enormous purchasing power of governments and local councils could be used to demand that contracts only be given to those firms who provide an effective equality programme for women within their organisations, providing both training and promotion. That this can be done has been illustrated by the activities of the Greater London Council (GLC). More effective use could be made of the powerful tool of financial pressure than is currently occurring. Similarly it is open to unions, in their negotiations, to press for more effective equality programmes and positive discrimination programmes within the organisations they deal with, whether in the private or public sector.

Whether, in fact, such actions will be undertaken is another matter. There are many reasons to suspect that they won't. Certainly in terms of politics the signs are inauspicious. The main parties are deeply divided ideologically but neither polarity seems likely to transform training in a way that assists women. The current Conservative Government embraces a political ideology which, however muted in practice, is certainly against the kind of governmental intervention that using the tool of contracts and finance to open up the labour market and training to women could ensure. Meanwhile it is under their authority that the existing state-funded training schemes are so limiting women's chances and allowing deep-rooted sexism to maintain its away. Deep suspicions also exist about the role of trade unions. Whilst unions have acted to look after the rights and expectations of workers, there are suspicions being voiced that in too many instances those workers are perceived only in male terms. In the unions the hierarchy of officials is overwhelmingly male and many commentators feel that both officials and union policies are riven by male interests, that they do not perceive problems or their solutions in terms of the interests of female workers. Wage demands, shorter working hours, low pay, are all union policy areas that have been criticised for the manner in which they have been handled by the unions, an approach inimicable to the needs of women (Coote and Campbell, 1982). For many male unionists women are seen as a threat, a perspective rooted in history, in the times when cheaper women workers were regarded as a possible replacement for more expensive skilled male labour. From this viewpoint women were a problem and a menace and they have never been successfully part of the mainstream of British trade unionism. Women are not now deliberately suppressed in or excluded from trade unions, but neither do they have access to equal positions of power and authority within the unions; and nor, as yet, do those unions fully reflect their needs. Many men would prefer to see the absence of female officials in unions today as a reflection of disinterest on the part of women. Other though, are beginning to recognise that there are connections between women's role in the home and their political and union absence. As a report for NUPE (National Union of Public Employees) argued:

> We do not believe that the under-representation has anything to do with 'women's nature' or lack of interest in the affairs of NUPE . . . It has to do first with the position of women in the wider society and in work. All women come through a process which emphasises domestic activity as a prime virtue, especially supportive of an secondary to the activities of men.
> (Quoted in Coote and Campbell, 1982, p. 161)

Or to put it in the words of a female shop steward:

> A lot of women have to go home and cook tea for their husbands. Or they can't go out because they've got to do their washing or their ironing.   (Coote and Campbell, 1982, p. 159)

However, if the majority of trade unions and trade unionists are firmly set within a male perspective and have failed to champion women's causes wholeheartedly so far, this does not mean that trade unions are entirely without the potentiality and possibilities that would mean that they could do so.

Women have made some inroads into the unions and won some gains there. The Trades Union Congress has a charter for equality and has embraced the principle, if not always the practice, of positive action for women. Individual unions have supported female members's complaints about the lack of equal pay, about grading, about unequal pension rights. They've pushed for maternity pay and supported cases taken on grounds of sex discrimination. Such individual moves are, at least, positive steps in relation to the overwhelmingly male domination of the union movement. The unions are also under increasing pressure from their female members to reflect on their own internal practices and policies in relation to women. Unions therefore retain a potential for action in this area but at the moment they are a far from effective force in the attempt to develop programmes and training which would open up opportunities to women.

What this discussion is attempting to illustrate, however, is not the fact that various political forces are reactionary or are failing to reach their potential; rather the aim is to illustrate how far we are from developing any really far-reaching definition of what training policy might involve and how it might be implemented. Neither the possible compensatory aspect nor the initiating aspect have really met with any serious consideration in Britain. Discussion at the moment remains tightly tied to the almost traditional view of training, based on a period of life, after schooling, mainly for men and rooted in the transmission of technical knowledge. In this respect we remain locked in our history and the potentiality of an aggressive and wide-ranging training policy which would embrace these aspects remains unexplored. Training remains a narrowly conceived form and as such retains all the aspects which mitigate most strongly against women's effective participation. It constrains the numbers entering, the types of occupations, and orientates most of its activities towards the young, many of whom, if female, may not have accurately realised their need for economic activity and the role a job will play in their future lives. A wider, far-reaching policy is required, for women – especially, but also for men. Not all men have the school experiences that give them access to the kind of opportunities they'd like, and the differential experience of various ethnic minority groups serves only to highlight such problems.

However, if this is the kind of training policy that we should demand be created, an active and invigorating one rather than reactive and limited, what about the kind of training facilities and programmes that we have for the moment? Clearly there are a number of problems involved which have produced the kind of discrimination in training that much of this book documents. For these quick, short-term solutions are possible although again they are far from inevitable. Already there are in existence in Britain training schemes aimed at women which try to come to terms with some of the issues that have been raised in this book. Yet these schemes are not to be found in the mainstream of training provision in Britain, but instead are often one-off schemes fuelled by the enthusiasm and initiative of groups of women around the country.

One of the first issues to be faced in the effective development of training for women, when that training takes place outside work, is how to get the women in. They won't come if they haven't heard about the schemes or had them presented in such a way as to make them seem viable, attractive possibilities. Advertising then becomes a priority but advertising where? What many of the more independent female-oriented groups have done is to go to where all kinds of women are likely to be found, in the supermarkets, in child health centres, in markets, community centres, and day care nurseries, all the places women will visit in the course of their day-to-day activities. This helps to ensure that women actually receive information about the courses and associate them with their day-to-day activities rather than see them as some rarefied activity taking place elsewhere. It's also possible to hold open days beforehand so that women can tentatively test the water rather than commit themselves at once.

Whilst some of the training opportunities that need to be opened to women do involve qualifications of a specific kind, as in banking for example, many other training opportunities can have the compensatory element as part of the main body of the course. In other words, if women need to know things they learn them on the course, it doesn't exclude them. A lack of formal pre-entry requirements is very important for many women, and is going to become very important in opening up opportunities to women from ethnic minority groups. Although many will do well in the British school system there is also evidence of deeply ingrained racism in many areas which works against an academically successful schooling. Other women may well have entered Britain as immigrants and again not have had the opportunity to acquire the language or schooling that existing courses require. In all circumstances like these the development of courses without formal education requirements is a major step in opening up opportunities:

> When I came to England from Pakistan in 1969, I couldn't speak a world of English. I learned to speak English and then I went to High School but I left before taking the CSE exams. Although may parents encouraged me to further education I had no interest in school . . . By 1982 I had three children and a husband to look after. At this time I saw a poster advertising the Leeds Women's Workshop. I couldn't believe that there could be free training for women like me in electronics and microcomputing, a subject I had grown to be inquisitive about.
>
> (Surya Ramzan, *Women and Training New* Spring 1985, p. 3).

A related issue to the one of open access through the removal of formal qualification barriers is that of priority. Should women or certain groups of women be given priority on training courses? Different groups have taken different decisions about this and in some ways this reflects the realities of local labour markets as well as consideration of the overall position of women in our society. We know that women in general tend to occupy positions at a lower level and with lower pay, but often there are groups of women whose position is, in general, even worse. Local choices then determine whose need is greatest and reflect local rather than national conditions. In the case of the East Leeds Women's Workshop that Surya trained with priority was given to women over 25 who lived in the area, were single parents, Black or Asian and/ or had no previous experience of further education. These priorities related to the location of the workshop in a community which was working class with large Afro-Caribbean and

Asian populations and where the textile industry – and many women's jobs with it – had gone into a decline and disappeared. The workshop therefore gave priority to the women of its area and by providing courses in carpentry and joinery, and electronics and microcomputing, orientated future opportunities for its entrants away from areas of declining job opportunity for women to where opportunities might open. As a result one woman who before the course spent her time 'looking after my daughter and sometimes I worked part time, cleaning or serving in a shop, – now finds herself in a totally different situation:

> I now work as a woodwork instructor in an activities centre for the unemployed. I run the workshop and assist and advise the users of the centre on the best way to make their projects. I am also doing a carpentry and joinery course at Leeds Building College on day release . . . I am really excited by my new trade and job.
>
> (Joyce, *Women and Training News*, Spring 1985, p. 3)

Finance is another important aspect, finance both for the trainees and for the workshop itself. Different workshops have different positions on this. The East Leed Women's Workshop, for instance, does not pay women for their participation but does give help with childcare and travel expenses. In the MSC schemes, on the other hand, training allowances are available. The question of how finance operates is, however, inevitably linked to other factors. Women may get allowances for attending state financed TOPS courses but childcare is not providing in any of the centres and women have to make their own arrangements, arrangements that cost money. Yet the South Glamorgan Women's Workshop has a purpose built nursery attached to it which provides free childcare. This sort of provision makes the training course accessible to many women who can happily make long-term commitments knowing that their children are taken care of and that there is no financial strain. Yet, as discussion of MSC provision has shown, one of the continual problems in MSC provision is the failure to provide any kind of child care facility even though staff on courses dealing with women are constantly emphasising its necessity.

It is at this point that the importance of finance for training provision becomes clear. With the MSC so resistant to many of the changes that would help women get easier access to training, it is in training provision outside this form of state funding that many initiatives are being undertaken. The sources of finance for training are varied. Some finance can come, for example, from local councils but an important supplement for training finance as regards women has come through the EEC. The European Economic Community may seem distant from the everyday concerns of many people but there is in existence the ESF, the European Social Fund, which whilst not large in comparison to some EEC budgets does possess financial resources that have helped women in Britain. The ESF is able to give money towards training projects and in order to do this equably has developed a system of priorities about the kind of training its limited resources will aid. For some years now these priorities have included the provision of training for women, especially those returning to work. A project has to get some public funding, but the ESF will then match that funding. This means, of course, that projects can get off the ground which it might otherwise be beyond the ability of a domestic British budget to afford. The South Glamorgan Women's Workshops, for instance, is funded by South Glamorgan County Council and the ESF; the East Leeds Women's Workshop gets its finance from Leeds City Council and the ESF. This also points to the importance of the local level once again. Undoubtedly the political affiliations of particular councils must help in generating decisions about such matters as assisting in the establishment of women's training workshops, but is also reflects the awareness of the particular problems and inadequacies of local labour markets, and the particular needs of local communities and groups of women. This is an awareness that does not appear to find expression through the structure of the MSC in any such forceful way. Meanwhile, the abolition of the Greater London Council and other metropolitan councils is removing one source of this alternative finance. The removal of these councils is merely one element in the overall tension between local and central government which has existed for decades. Yet, as far as women are concerned the general swing in favour of centralisation is to be regretted because it is the local authorities that have done the most to pressurise for effective alternatives for women and provided the necessary finance, whilst central agencies, such as the MSC, have been consistently criticised for their failure to make effective use of the specific priorities of the ESF in relation to women (WEDG, Women and the MSC, undated).

If ways of getting women into courses can be simply and speedily developed by the rearrangement of finance or by the provision of facilities such as childcare which lighten both the financial and domestic burden, are other aspects of training so easily altered?

One element that could be changed is that of age. Many of the training opportunities that do exist are aimed at those who have just finished school and this is itself is a reflection of historical experience. Schools were regarded as providing education, which was seen as different from training which provided technical knowledge. Therefore training was provided after schools as a process of acquisition of the forms of knowledge appropriate to the world of work. This was a view of working life that presumed a long, probably permanent experience of a particular occupation. Yet although there have been many calls for 'continuing education; and expressions of belief that many people will now have to change jobs (if they can get employment) several times in their working life, it still remains the case that much training is still targeted at school leavers. In some cases, as with the MSC, this is rooted in a belief that somehow school leavers could get work, that what they lack is some element that makes them unemployable for the moment and which can be compensated for. This may or may not have been the case when the MSC was set up but it is far from being true today, when television newscasts broadcast daily the number of job losses over the country. Yet, for women, the question of the age at which training is targeted is important. Even if we build a compensatory element into training, many girls will leave school envisaging early marriage and a family and therefore having little interest in training. If they do take up training opportunities and these are not provided as women-only courses then female entrants may have a severe testing, socially and personally as well as technically. This has led at least one woman trainer in an electrical and electronic engineering department to say that moves should be made to work with older women, not those straight from school:

> Problems are much more acute for a 16-year-old. The 16-year-old boys she is working with are likely to be very insecure about their own sexuality. The worst insult they can call each other is 'cow' or 'slag' or 'poufta' or 'woman'. The 16-year-old girl herself is likely to be coming to terms with her own sexuality. She is bombarded with messages from society saying that to be attractive to men she must conform to certain stereotypes, wear certain clothes, move in a certain way, be disarmingly hopeless at technical work. In order to succeed at work or college she requires a self-confidence about her own capabilities that runs contra to these images. . .advantage of training older women is that they are likely to be much more able to cope with the pressures of the situation. They can genuinely laugh off the 16-year-old boys. They are also likely to have much more motivation for learning. Although studying may be a problem at first, they will be able to stand the pressures and are better motivated to complete the training and once there is a group of women working and training on building sites, in factories, in technical colleges, then the choice of career or training becomes a much more realistic one for a 16-year-old girl.   (J. Tizard, 1984)

A further major obstacle must be the question of who train the trainers. In many cases, especially in the non-centrally state-aided course, attempts have been made to get female trainers to teach other women. This has not always been easy, especially when the areas involved have been precisely those ones that have had very few women in them. By far the largest majority of those who train women or who assess their eligibility for courses are men and the evidence from all areas and across countries suggests the deep, intransigent sexism of many of those involved. This is, of course, a problem in all levels of education as well as in training but it is a problem that seems unlikely to change unless a rigorous and determined effort is made to check it. Upon changes there, however,

depend many of the other points that have come to light over
the previous chapters. The changing of teaching methods, the
assessment of the curriculum, of its phrasing and timing, are
all unlikely to occur unless those involved are aware of there
being a problem which something has to be done about. This
obviously indicates the need to introduce training in awareness of such issues and the consistent evaluation of attempts to
open up opportunities to women. If this is the case, then it
seems to point in the direction of explicit positive action
programmes where the setting up of goals and timetables,
together with effective monitoring, is central to their
successful implementation.

However, it is precisely the area of establishing goals and
timetables that research has shown to be a most contentious
issue (Povall, 1984). This is partly because of general social
attitudes which bear with them the unwillingness to actively
fight for equality for women, but also because the setting up of
such programmes is seen as unsurping some of the rights of
management itself, whether this is in the private or the public
sector:

> The setting of targets to increase the number of women pro-
> moted into jobs in which they are under-represented is the
> centrepiece of American affirmative action programmes. In
> Europe, goals or targets are confused with quotas and some
> managers assume that by setting targets they will have to give
> jobs to unsuitable candidates. Others reject targets as alien to
> their way of managing. Some of the resistance arises because
> initially it is difficult to set realistic ones. But for others targets
> or goals are seen as inappropriate because they represent a
> serious results-oriented programme with connotations of
> long-term commitment.   (Povall, 1984, p. 39)

In many cases programmes like these have only been introduced where there are female-intensive institutions and large-
scale employers who pride themselves on their personnel
policies. If positive action were to be more widely implemented are would have to do more than merely wait on the
generous actions of particular employers. One study has suggested two ways of increasing positive action programmes.
The first, which we have already considered in relation to

training, is through the use of financial pressure, by making such positive action programmes a requirement for the receipt of government contracts. The second way of increasing the programmes could be through the development of the Equal Opportunity Commission's powers so that the EOC used its existing powers more vigorously and received the additional power, backed up by the courts, of ensuring its recommendations made an employer change practices (Robarts, 1981).

> We would like to see a Positive Action Resolution included in all government contracts where the contractor employs more than a minimum number of people. The Resolution would require the employer to negotiate and adopt a positive action programme which would involve analysing the workforce to identify the jobs in which women . . . were under-represented and drawing up a detailed programme to remedy the situation. In order to be effective, a clause of this kind in the contract would have to be closely monitored to ensure the employers were taking their duties seriously: We propose that the Equal Opportunities Commission should be given the job of monitoring such clauses and their implementation. If the employer refuses to negotiate such a positive action agreement, or the agreement is inadequate or is not being implemented, the EOC should be able to apply to the CAC (Central Arbitration Committee) for a ruling directing the employer to negotiate and/or implement a positive action programme and, if necessary, modifying the terms of the agreed programme. Similarly a trade union should have the power to complain to the CAC if the employers refused to negotiate or implement the agreement, as should an individual woman.   (Robarts, 1981, p. 94)

Such changes would obviously do a great deal to alter the prospects for women within firms and organisations, and enable them to take full advantage of the internal labour markets and training openings that are located there. Positive action could also be applied equally as effectively in training schemes, ensuring that women had access to the programmes and were not subject to discrimination within them. It would also be an important way, as it has been in the USA, of tackling the issue of racial discrimination. Effective monitoring would at least be step towards developing realisation of the double burden which many women from different ethnic groups suffer.

All of these changes, whether they involve a radical rethinking of what we mean by training and when, where and how, this takes place, or whether it involves a more effective adjustment of existing schemes to help suit women, require an impetus. The question is whether this will come. At first sight the problem seems to resolve itself into one of policy making *per se*. That is to say, can we change the attitudes of those in charge in such a way as to give full value to the needs of women? However, an analysis that rests just on attitude changes merely touches the surface because it ignores the fact that in many ways men materially benefit from the subordinate position of women. Political parties, trade unions, even the MSC are not gender-neutral bodies. In our society they are dominated numerically by men who, following the general labour market trends, occupy the major positions of authority. In wanting changes in training policies and training schemes we are asking for changes which will directly affect the prospects and experiences of many men. Employers, predominantly male, have directly profited from the subordinate position of women in the labour market, whether in terms of wage rates, or less calculable effects like the availability and preference of women with children for forms of part-time or home work. Unions, again dominated by men, have failed to effectively represent and fight for the interests of women. In employment men have had promotion and career paths open to them because women have been effectively barred from these experiences. Meanwhile men, as men, have benefited from the focus of women on the home and the fact that women in paid employment still find it necessary to take on most of the responsibility for household tasks.

Elements in this picture are currently under attack. In some areas of Britain such as Wales, more women than men seem likely to be in paid employment by 1990 (Williams, 1982) and this obviously has repercussions in areas such as unionisation. It seems likely that the development of such patterns will work to make unions more aware and more responsive to women's needs. However, the unions will be forced by circumstances into this position and what is happening in South Wales is not necessarily what is happening elsewhere. The impact of opening up 'non-traditional' job opportunities and providing career paths in institutions such as banks and building societies seems likely to provoke grave antagonism in men. In our current and likely future economy where the number of jobs is not expanding rapidly opening up areas to women means closing them down for men. If women get effective rights the 'job in the bank' is no longer going to necessarily provide the unbroken path of opportunity it now offers to so many men. Such circumstances seem likely to increase antagonism between men and women. An effective training policy for women requires effective changes at many levels. If it requires what are regarded as 'sacrifices' by men how easily is such a transition to be achieved? From this perspective any gains at all must be counted as victories and there appears little likelihood that the struggle to achieve training opportunities for women will reach its conclusion in the immediate future.

Postscript

Undoubtedly by the time this book reaches the bookshops there will have been some changes. Already there are signs that the MSC, for instance, is introducing changes in relation to the financing of certain courses in FE colleges that will affect the amount of autonomy local authorities have over training provision. Also a two year YTS is to be introduced. What is unlikely to change, however, are the forms of discrimination which women suffer from in training processes. The structures may shift and change, taking new forms, but it seems that the effects of those structures are unlikely to alter so far as women go. Any changes that have occurred should therefore be subjected to the kind of scrutiny that I have tried to give existing training provision.

One excellent way of keeping in touch with changes in training and with research on this topic is through *Women and Training News*. This is available from:

The Editor,
GLOSCAT,
Oxstalls Lane,
Gloucester GL2 9HW.

Select Bibliography

A New Training Initiative, Dec. 1981, Cmnd 8455, HMSO.

Alexander, M. (1979), *Equal Opportunities and Vocational Training*, Berlin, CEDEFOP.

Allum, C. and Quigley, J. (1983), 'Bricks in the Wall: The Youth Training Scheme', *Capital and Class*, Winter.

Amos, V. and Parmar, P. (1981), 'Resistance and Responses: The Experience of Black Girls in Britain', in A. McRobbie and T. McCabe (eds), *Adventure Stories for Girls*, London, RKP.

Ardron, R. (–) WEP9 Newsletter, No. 1, mimeograph.

Avis, J. (1983), 'Selection and Differentiation in Further Education, in D. Gleeson (ed.), *Youth Training and the Search for Work*, London, RKP.

Bates, I. *et al.*, (1984), *Schooling for the Dole*, London, Macmillan.

Beechey, V. (1982), 'The Sexual Division of Labour and the Labour Process: A Critical Review of Braverman', in S. Woods (ed.), *The Degradation of Work*, London, Hutchison.

Beechey, V. (1983), 'Whats' so Special about Women's Employment?' *Feminist Review*, No. 15.

Bergmann, B. and Darity, W. (1981), 'Social Relations, Productivity and Employer Discrimination', *Monthly Labour Review*, Vol. 104, Pt. 4.

Berner, B. (1983), 'Women, Power and Ideology in Technical Education and Work', mimeograph.

Blunden, G. (1983), 'Typing in the Tech', in D. Gleeson (ed.), *Youth Training and the Search For Work*, London, RKP.

Bradshaw, P. and Laidlaw, C. (1979), *Women in Engineering*, Watford, EITB.

Brah, A. (1978), 'Age, Race and Power Relations: The Case of South Asian Youth in Britain', in M. Day and D. Marsland, *Black Kids, White Kids, What Hope?*, Leicester: National Youth Bureau.

Braybon, G. (1982), 'The Need for Women's Labour in the First World War', in E. Whitelegg *et al.* (eds), *The Changing Experience of Women*, London, Martin Robertson.

Brelsford, P. (et al 1982), *Give Us A Break*, Research and Development Series, No. 11, Sheffield, MSC.

Brelsford, P. (1983), 'Equal Opportunity in Training Programmes?', *Women and Training News*, No. 11.

135

Breughel, I. (1979), 'Women as a Reserve Army of Labour', *Feminist Review*, No. 3.

Carby, C. (1982), 'Schooling in Babylon', in CCCS, *The Empire Strikes Back*, London, Hutchinson.

CCCS (1981), *Unpopular Education*, London, Hutchison.

Cockburn C., (1981), 'The Material of Male Power', *Marxism Today*, No. 9.

Cockburn, C. (1983), *Brothers*, London, Pluto.

Cockburn, C. (1983b), 'Caught in the Wheels', *Marxism Today*, Nov. 1983.

Cockburn, C. (1984), 'Women and Technology: Opportunity is Not Enough', mimeograph. BSA Conference.

Coote A, and Campbell, B. (1982), *Sweet Freedom*, London, Picador.

Coyle, A. (1982), 'Sex and Skill in the Organisation of the Clothing Industry;, in J. West (ed.) *Work, Women and the Labour Market*, London, Routledge & Kegan Paul.

Coyle, A. (1984), *Redundant Women*, London, Women's Press.

Commission for Racial Equality (–), *Looking for Work*, London, CRE.

Crompton, R. and Jones, G. (1984), *White-collar Proletariat: De-skilling and Gender in Clerical Work*, London, Macmillan.

Cross, M. (1982) 'The Manufacture of Marginality, by E. Cashmore and B. Troyna (eds) *Black Youth in Crisis*, London: George Allen & Unwin.

Davvies, B. (1982), *The State We're In*, Occasional Paper No. 2, The National Youth Bureau.

Davies, S. (1983), 'YTS (–) Equality of Opportunity?' *Women and Training News*, No. 13.

Deem, R. (1978), *Women and Schooling*, London, Routledge & Kegan Paul.

Deem, R. (1980), *Schooling for Women's Work*, London Routledge & Kegan Paul.

Deem, R. (1984) *Co-education Reconsidered*, Milton Keynes, OU Press.

Dex, S, (1983), 'The Second Generation: West Indian Female School Leavers', in A. Phizacklea, *One Way Ticket: Migration and Female Labour*, London, Routledge & Kegan Paul.

Dex, S. (1983b), 'Second Chances: Further Education, Ethnic Minorities' in D. Gleeson (ed.), *Youth Training and the Search for Work*, London, Routledge & Kegan Paul.

Downing, H. (1980), 'Word Processors and the Oppression of Woman', in T. Forrester (ed.) *The Microelectronics Revolution*, Oxford, Basil Blackwell.

Driver, G. (1980), 'How West Indians do better at School, *New Society*, Vol. 51, No. 902.

Egan, A. (1982), 'Women in Banking – a Study of Inequality' *Industrial Relations Journal*, Vol. 13, No. 3, Autumn.

EMCO, (1982), 'Training or Job Substitution?', *Forum*, Vol. 25, No. 1.

EOC, (1981), *Annual Report*

EOSYS (1984), *Case Studies in Information Technology and Career Opportunities' for Women*, Sheffield MSC.

EPOS (1982), 'New Technology and Women's Employment,' *Social Change and Technology in Europe Information Bulletin*, No. 5, Commission of the European Communities, 1982.

Farish, M. (1984), *The Youth Training Scheme: A Critical Response*, mimeograph. BSA Conference.

Fairley, J. (1982), 'The Great Training Robbery', *Marxism Today*, November.

Fairley, J. (1983–4), 'The YTS and Democracy', *Youth and Policy*, Vol. 2 No. 3.

Finn, D. (1983), 'The Youth Training Scheme: A New Deal', *Youth and Policy*, Vol. 1, No. 4.

Finn, D. (1984), 'Britain's Misspent Youth', *Marxism Today*, February.

Ford, J., Keil, T., Bryman, A., Beardsworth, A. (1984), 'Internal Labour Market Processes', *Industrial Relations Journal*, Vol. 15, No. 2, Summer.

Fuller, M (1982), 'Young, Female and Black', in E. Cashmore and B. Troyna (eds.) *Black Youth in Crisis*, London, Allen & Unwin.

Fuller, M. (1980), 'Black Girls in a London Comprehensive School' in R. Deem (ed.), *Schooling for Women's work*, London, Routledge & Kegan Paul.

Gale, K. and Marks, P. (1984), 'Twentieth-century Trends in the Work of Women in England and Wales', *J.R. Statistical Society*, Vol. 137, Part 1.

Game, A. and Pringle, R. (1984), *Gender at Work*, London, Pluto Press.

Gleeson, D. (1983), *Youth Training and the Search for Work*, London, Routledge & Kegan Paul.

Golubeva, V. (1984) 'In the North Provinces', in T, Mamanova (ed.) *Women and Russia*, Oxford, Basil Blackwell.

Greater London Training Board (1984), *The New Training Initiative, 1981–1984*, London, GLC.

Griffiths, M. (1980), 'Women in Higher Education: A Case Study of the Open University', in R. Deem (ed.), *Schooling for Women's Work* London, Routledge & Kegan Paul.

Hakim, C. (1981), 'Job Segregation: Trends in the 1970s', *Employment Gazette*, December.

Harber, J. (1983) 'A New Insight', *Women and Training News*, No. 11.

Hoskyns, C. (1985), 'Women's Equality and the European Communities', *Feminist Review*, No. 20.

House of Commons Expenditure Committee (1973), *The Employment of Women, Sixth Report*, London, HMSO.

House of Commons Expenditure Committee (1973b), *Seventh Report* London, HMSO.

Huws, U. (1982), *Your Job in the Eighties*, London, Pluto Press.

Jamcar, B. (1978), *Women Under Communism*, London, The John Hopkins Press.

Kumar, K. (1978), *Prophesy and Progress*, London, Penguin.

Khan, V.S. (1979), 'Work and Network: South Asian Women in South London', in Wallman S. (ed.) *Ethnicity at Work*, London, Macmillan.

Lapidus, G. (1978), *Women in Soviet Society*, University of California, Press.

Leeds Trade Union and Community Resource and Information Centre (1982), *New Technology and Women's Employment*, Manchester, EOC.

Lewisham Women and Employment Project (1982), *Women and Training: Who Said opportunities?*, London, Lewisham Women and Employment Group.

Liljestrom, R. et al (1978), *Roles in Transition*, Stockholm, Liber Forlag.

Lovell, A. (1980), 'Fresh Horizons for Some', *Adult Education*, Vol. 53, No. 4.

McNally, J. and Shimmin, S. (1984), 'Job Evaluation and Equal Pay for work of Equal Value', *Personnel Review*, Vol. 13, No. 1.

Mamanova, T. (1984), *Women and Russia*, Oxford, Basil Blackwell.

Martin, J. and Roberts, C. (1984), *Women and Employment: A Liftime Perspective*, London, HMSO.

Massey, D. (1983), 'The Shape of Things to Come', *Marxism Today*, April.

Mayo, M. (1983), 'Rejoinder to Teresa Perkins', in M. Evans and C. Ungerson (eds.)

Sexual Divisions, Patterns and Processes, London, Tavistock.

Meehan, E. (1983), 'Equal Opportunity Policies: Some Implications for Women of Contrasts between Enforcement Bodies in Britain and the USA', in M.J. Lewis (ed.) *Women's Welfare, Women's Rights*, London, Croom Helm.

Michaels, R. (1973), *New Opportunities for Women*, Occasional Papers of Hatfield Poly, No. 1.

Millman, V. (1984), *The New Vocationalism in Schools and its Influence on Girls*, unpublished paper, Girl-Friendly Schooling Conference, Manchester.

Moos, M. (1983), 'The Training Myth: A Critique of the Government's Response to Youth Employment and its Impact on Further Education', in D. Gleeson (ed.) *Youth Training and the Search for Work*, London, Routledge & Kegan Paul.

Moos, M. (1983), 'How Far Further for Further Education', *Youth and Policy*, Vol. 2. No. 1.

Moss, P. (1980), 'Parents at Work', in P. Moss and N. Fonda (eds.), *Work and the Family*, London, Temple Smith.

Morgan, J. (1981), 'Typing our Way to Freedom', *Feminist Review*, No. 9.

Mosco, V. (1982), *Pushbutton Fantasies: Critical Perspectives on Videotex and Information Technology*, New Jersey, Ablex Publishing Corporation.

MSC (1976), *Training Opportunities for Women*, London, MSC.

MSC (1977), *Young People and Work*, London, MSC.

MSC (1979), *Opportunities for Girls and Women in the MSC Special Programmes for the Unemployed*, London, MSC.

Network Training Group (1983), *Training and the State*, Manchester, Network Training Group.

Newton, P. (1981), *Getting on in Engineering*, mimeograph.

Oakley, A. (1981), *Subject Women*, London, Martin Robertson.

O'Connor, M. (1984), 'Going Into Training', *Guardian*, October 23.

Pahl, R. (1984), *The Divisions of Labour*, Oxford, Basil Blackwell.

Parmar, P. (1982), 'Gender, Race and Class: Asian Women in Resistance', in LCC's Race and Politics Group, *The Empire Strikes Back*, London, Hutchinson.

Patritti-Jagger, P. (1983), 'Women can be Managers', *Women and Training News*, No. 11.

Perkins, T. (1983), 'A New Form of Employment', in M. Evans and C. Ungerson (eds.), *Sexual Divisions, Patterns and Processes*, London, Tavistock.

Perry, P. (1976), *The Evolution of British Manpower Policy*, London, BACIE.

Phillips, A. (1983), *Hidden Hands*, London, Pluto Press.

Phillips, A. and Taylor, B. (1980), 'Sex and Skill', *Feminist Review*, No. 6.

Phizacklea, A. (1982), 'Migrant Women and Wage Labour: The Case of West Indian Women in Britain' in J. West (ed.) *Work, Women and the Labour Market*, London Routledge & Kegan Paul.

Pollert, A. (1981), *Girls, Wives, Factory Lives*, London, Macmillan.

Povall, M. (1984), 'Overcoming Barriers to Women's Advancement in European Organisations', *Personnel Review*, Vol. 13, No. 1.

Povall, M., de Jong, A. *et al.*, (1982), 'Banking on Women Managers', *Management Today*, February.

Randall, V. (1982), *Women and Politics*, London, Macmillan.

Rees, T. (1983), 'Boys off the Street and Girls in the Home: Youth Unemployment and State Intervention in Northern Ireland', in R. Fiddy (ed.) *In Place of Work*, Falmer, Falmer Press.

Rees, T. (1984), *Reproducing Gender Inequality in the Labour Force: The Role of the State*, Standing Conference of the Sociology of Further Education, Paper No. 84/27e.

Rees, T. and Gregory, D. (1981), 'Youth Employment and Unemployment: A Decade of Doctrine', *Educational Analysis*, Vol. 3, No. 2.

Rees, G. and Rees, T. (1982), *Youth Unemployment and State Intervention*, London Routledge & Kegan Paul.

Robarts, S. (1981), *Positive Action for Women*, London, NCCL.

Robins, K. and Webster, F. (1982), 'New Technology: A Survey of Trade Union Response in Britain', *Industrial Relations Journal*, Vol 13, No. 1, Spring.

Rothwell, S. (1980), 'United Kingdom', in A. Yohalem (ed.) *Women Returning to Work*, London, Frances Pinter.

Row Europe (1983), *Women's Rights and the EEC*, London, ROW.

Sammons, P. (1983), 'Patterns of Participation in Vocational Further Education', in D. Gleeson (ed.) *Youth Training and the Search for Work*, London Routledge & Kegan Paul.

Scott, Hilda (1982), *Sweden's Right to be Human*, London, Allison & Busby.

Sharp, B. (1984), *Computer Technology and its Impact on Women's Employment*, unpublished paper, Girl – Friendly Schooling Conference, Manchester.

Shaw, J. (1984), 'The Politics of Single-sex Schools', in R. Deem (ed.) *Co-education Reconsidered*, Milton Keynes, Open University Press.

Sheffield Trades Council (1982), 'Trade Union Response to YOPS and NTI', Mimeograph.

Smith, S. (1984) 'Single-Sex Setting', in R. Deem (ed), *Co-Education Reconsidered*, Milton Keynes, OU Press.

Snell, M. (1979) 'The Equal Pay and Sex Discrimination Acts' *Feminist Review*, No. 1.

SPRU (1982), *Microelectronics and Women's Employment in Britain*, University of Sussex, SPRU.

Stantonbury Campus (Briddewater Hall) Sexism in Education Group (1984), 'The realities of mixed schooling', in R. Deem (ed.), *Co-education Reconsidered*, Milton Keynes, Open University Press.

Stoney, S. (1984), 'Girls entering Science and Technology: The Problems and Possibilities for Action as Viewed from the FE Perspective*, mimeograph. Girl – Friendly Schooling Conference, Manchester.

Stoney, S. and Reid, M. (1981), *Further Opportunities in Focus*, FE Unit, London.

Solomos, J. (1983), *The Politics of Black Unemployment*, Birmingham.

Solomos, J. (1984) *Problems, but whose problems? The Social Construction of Black Youth Unemployment and State Policies* mimeograph.

Swann Report, DES 1985, Education for all: report of the Committee of Enquiry into the education of children from ethnic minorities, Cmnd 9453, HMSO.

Swarbrick, A. (1982), 'Technology – Overcoming the Career Break', Women and Training News, Issue 9.

Thompson, J. (1983), *Learning Liberation: Women's Response to Men's Education*, London, Croom Helm.

Tizard, J. (1984), *Positive Action in Technician Training*, mimeograph. Girl – Friendly Schooling Conference, Manchester.

Ward, R. (1984), *Girls in Technology*, unpublished paper, Girl – Friendly Schooling Conference, Manchester.

Watts, A.G. (1983), *Education, Unemployment and the Future of Work*, Milton

Keynes, Open University Press.

Webster, J. (1984), *Word Processing and the Secretarial Labour Process*, mimeograph.

Werneke, D. (1983), *Microelectronics and Office Jobs*, International Labour Office, Geneva.

West, J. (1982), 'New Technology and Women's Office Work, in J. West (ed.) *Work, Women and the Labour Market*, London Routledge & Kegan Paul.

Wickham, A. (1982), 'The State and Training Programmes for Women', in E. Whitelegg *et al.*, (ed.) *The Changing Experience of Women*, London, Martin Robertson.

Wilkins, P. (1983), 'Women and Engineering in the Plymouth Area: Job Segregation and Training at Company Level', *EOC Research Bulletin*, No. 7, Summer.

Williams, G. (1982), 'Land of Our Fathers', *Marxism Today*, Vol. 26, No. 8.

Willis, P. (1977), *Learning to Labour*, Guildford, Saxon House.

Women's National Commission (1984), 'Conference Papers', mimeograph.

Woodhall, M. (1973) 'Investment in Women: A Reappraisal of the Concept of Human Capital', *International Review of Education*, Vol. 19, No. 1.

Youthaid (1984), *The Youth Training Scheme*, London, Youthaid.

Youthaid (1981) *Quality or Collapse, Youthaid Review of Yop*. London, Youthaid.

Youthaid (1984b) Press Release, Feb. 13.

Youth Task Group (1982), *Report*, London, MSC.

Young, David (1982), 'Worried about unemployment? How You Can Help. . .', *The Director*, October.

Index